IN VINO VERITAS

A Guide for Hoteliers and Restaurateurs to Sell More Wine

By

Adam Mogelonsky & Larry Mogelonsky

Illustrated by Maureen Wright

authorHOUSE®

AuthorHouse™
1663 Liberty Drive
Bloomington, IN 47403
www.authorhouse.com
Phone: 833-262-8899

Published by AuthorHouse 08/30/2022

ISBN: 978-1-6655-6961-3 (sc)
ISBN: 978-1-6655-6960-6 (e)

IN VINO VERITAS

A Guide for Hoteliers and Restaurateurs to Sell More Wine

By

Adam Mogelonsky & Larry Mogelonsky

Illustrated by Maureen Wright

authorHOUSE®

AuthorHouse™
1663 Liberty Drive
Bloomington, IN 47403
www.authorhouse.com
Phone: 833-262-8899

Published by AuthorHouse 08/30/2022

ISBN: 978-1-6655-6961-3 (sc)
ISBN: 978-1-6655-6960-6 (e)

ALSO BY THE AUTHORS

More Hotel Mogel (2020)
The Hotel Mogel (2018)
The Llama is Inn (2017)
Hotel Llama (2015)
Llama Rules (2013)
Are You an Ostrich or a Llama? (2012)

This book is dedicated to our friends who
share this incredible wine journey:

Keith Edwards
always interested in finding an unusual wine to test and compare

Kevin Haverty Jr.
our expert in Californian Cabernet Sauvignon and Oregon Pinot Noir

Dale Jeffries
searching for and promoting any local success story

Alvin Nirenberg
the commensurate Bordeaux connoisseur

Klaus Tenter
who can be counted on to furnish incredible wines for our pleasure

James Tenute
who reminds us that there is no such thing as a bad time to consume a
glass or two

CONTENTS

FOREWORD

"Wine is sunlight held together by water."
– Galileo Galilei

From Josef Wagner

When you reflect on the most important and memorable meals of your life, what comes to mind? What do you truly remember?

Wine is as storied as human history, dating back to its origination nearly 9,000 years ago and has since had the influence to connect humanity beyond just historic facts. When we celebrate amongst family, friends or business partners, the one meal component that is important and memorable is the wine selection. From political conversations and scientific revelations to global business decisions, technological advancements, and even garnered stories that have been passed down through generations, wine has played a collaborative role in bringing people together. It's all about connection, a vital human need.

One of my favorite aspects of wine is how it lends itself to storytelling, an original form of communication and an ideal way to start or engage in conversation. Discussion topics can range from a dissection of tasting notes, how a particular wine is made, where it is from, when it was produced and details on the winemaker. We as hospitality professionals long for stories that spark our inner passion and desire to learn more, and the production of wine satisfies that need in an extraordinary way.

Similar to the happiness we feel when telling or listening to stories, wine brings us an internal joy and comfort. It creates a warm and cozy feeling and has the ability to transcend a mood, from relaxation to euphoria. When paired with food correctly, wine accentuates flavors, adds acidity, supports digestion and provokes deep thought.

Individual preferences play a large role when deciding on a wine pairing for a meal. In the industry we often see wine selections based on a guest and their food choices. However, the best restaurant experiences occur when the master sommelier selects highly allocated wines first. Once selected, the chef prepares a meal based on the flavor profile of the wines. I highly recommend going this route on your next epicurean adventure.

Wine is the most important part of a meal. It is the thread that ties the entire dining experience together from beginning to end, and is a vehicle to spark creativity, bring friends and strangers together, ignite passions and create memories for a lifetime. For your next meal, pour yourself a glass and enjoy the journey!

From Svetlana Atcheva

It is often both assumed and said that one needs guidance in choosing wine. I do believe that to be true. The question, however, is who or what you can trust to be your guide. I am here to say you do not need anyone or anything outside of the bottle of wine you're enjoying, your curiosity and your own palate.

The wine industry is complex and multilayered, and the journeys of each bottle from the vine to your table can be exceedingly diverse. Of course, there's the question of origin and grape varieties – that in and of itself can be a mind-numbingly confusing universe. Then, there's the question of producer – their ethos and techniques. Did your wine come from a million-litres tank, and on its way there (and after), never encountered human hands? Or did it come from a small cellar in a region you had never heard of, then was nursed throughout its life by the caresses of human attention?

Add to these the complexities of the business of wine – extremely different production costs across many regions along with different marketing budgets (or the absence of a marketing budget altogether), tariffs and taxes. And, please, do not forget the reputation and the popularity of the estates – often, but certainly, not necessarily connected. Human tastes accounting for the popularity of something are fluid and often change. A style of wine that was popular 20 years ago now can be something most people look at with derision. Similarly, reputations built on generations of expertise observing the same principles can no longer hold true if a new generation suddenly decides to change course or is simply not as observant or talented as its predecessors.

It is hard keeping up with all this information or attempting to hold it front of mind when you simply want to choose a wonderful bottle to accompany your meal at a restaurant. That is where the sommelier comes in the picture – a wine professional that one hopes can provide the guidance needed in the moment. Often however, and unfortunately so, this potentially useful exchange whose main purpose is to amplify and enrich the customer's experience takes the form of a lecture or a recitation of the sommelier's data knowledge about the region or the producer. It becomes yet another addition to the mishmash of complexities quoted above. None of this is necessary or helpful in any way.

Sommeliers are the last link in the chain of a wine's journey from vine to someone's table. It is always a long, complex voyage with a thousand human stories, discoveries and heartbreaks, trials and tribulations, distressing and sometimes tragic weather events or fairy tales of a growing seasons all woven together. The wine has these in its bones as well as the results from the decisions its caretakers took along the path. No sommelier can ever live through what a winemaker goes through on a yearly basis. This is not their job.

That being said, reciting a list of facts about percentages of new oak or a painstaking breakdown of the topographical complexities of a region is not the job either. The goal of every wine professional should be to carry the stories of the people whose hands made it and to comprehend the spirit that informs these individuals' visions of beauty. It is to try to grasp the relationship these growers have with their environments.

Lecturing about the rest – facts, labels, regions or production technicalities – is simply reducing wine to a compilation of details. Of course, these are useful to know when you sit around the table with other wine professionals and try to use this information as a tool to further your capacity for seeing deeper into wine.

It is my firm belief, however, that the cultivation of one's skills should be for the purpose of attempting to glimpse wine's hidden pleasures and to coax out the beginnings of knowledge about the bottle's true identity. And then, to connect it with the desires of a customer. It is only this ability – to see the spirit of the wine that answers the desire of a person then subside into the background – that makes one a true sommelier, a deliverer and a magician.

THE BASICS OF
SELLING WINE

*Out of respect for the innumerable people throughout
civilized history who have devoted themselves to the
craft of alcohol production, all specific beverage names
and grape varietals in this book are capitalized.*

The Fundamentals

Discussing specific grapes, growing regions or factoids related to wine, our aim is to give you some more worldly background information on viticulture so that you could better entice consumers towards a purchase. Talking about wine over food with friends and colleagues over the years, what becomes quite apparent is that people who work in the restaurant or hotel business have vastly superior wine knowledge than the layman. Many people couldn't tell the difference in taste between a Cabernet Sauvignon and a Merlot. For them, it's just red or white, or, if the time is right, sparkling white.

How then do you get the upsell? How do you convince a patron to go from drinking by the glass to purchasing a bottle for a table? How do you get someone to opt for one of the more expensive listings instead of the cheapest red on the menu?

When we're dining out at a table of four, it's easy for us to go through two bottles. When ordering the second one, we'll try something a tad more esoteric merely out of curiosity about the varietal's unique flavor profile and the country of origin. For someone without this ardent oenophilic fervor, what drives them to purchase a second bottle at a 300% markup (or more)?

Wine is a good business for all restaurants (or it should be!) to be in, and most of that lofty markup helps cover the sunk costs of operating that the food simply can't. But customers don't see those hidden costs, nor do they care. All they see is an exorbitant price tag on the menu. It's your job to justify that price tag by clearly explaining the benefits through a narrative about the unique qualities of each bottle's color, taste, history, geographic, pairing complements and so on.

Think of it as *tableside content marketing*. Any time that you educate a consumer on wine, you are giving them value in the same way as posting a blog entry to your website. You're proffering a gift while also demonstrating yourself as the expert. The key is to not overwhelm with too much information all at once – just enough to plant the seed. Knowing that this tableside marketing is what will enhance your wine revenues, there are two areas to focus on: your servers and your wine list.

Any good restaurateur will tell you that a server is only as good as his or her personality. A waiter can have all the food knowledge in the world, but if they can't convey that in an appealing tone then it's practically worthless. That said, knowledge is a close second. Not wherewithal specific to viticulture, but rather street smarts – being able to read a table and know the appropriate times to inject a few facts into the conversation or how to correctly prompt customers during the process of ordering.

Have your servers open with questions somewhere along the lines of, "Have you considered a bottle of wine for the table?" or "Do you need help with your selection?" Unless the patrons give your servers a hard 'no', chances are they already have a preference in mind, or they haven't made up their minds and could use some assistance.

From there, ask follow-up questions as opposed to insisting on one choice or another. "Can you narrow it down to white or red?" or, "Are you looking for a wine that best pairs with your mains?" Then you can get more specific with questions like, "Do you have a specific grape in mind?" or, "Can I help you choose a bottle from a particular country of origin?" At each juncture, servers can sprinkle in some morsels of information to create trust and bridge to the next question, making them all *mini sommeliers* in this regard.

It's these morsels of information are our focus for this book. Only we prefer a more colorful term to describe them – *wine stories* – because it's not disjoined facts that will help you sell products but the narrative that combines these morsels into a vivid account for easy cranial digestion.

And these wine stories should be readily apparent in how your wine selection is portrayed on the menu. Keep it simple and well-organized – that is, digestible. Instead of organizing the list by color then price, try arranging bottles by tasting notes and by suggested pairings. Moreover, be authentic and congruent with your selection. For example, if it's an Italian restaurant, specialize in Italian wine. (This sounds obvious, but in our experience, not always the case.)

Our wish with this book is for you to sell more wine at your restaurant, be it stand alone, chain or part of a hotel. If you apply the knowledge here and educate your staff appropriately, there's no reason why you shouldn't be able to sell two bottles or more per table at dinnertime.

A Checklist

Let's dedicate this chapter to those outlets that have the basics covered and are a few categories higher in their presentation of wine as an important component of their F&B mix.

As a caveat, this isn't intended for those five-star properties or haute cuisine outlets catering to wine gurus. Similarly, it isn't meant for those properties with wine lists scribed in gold leaf, leather-bound volumes which require three stevedores to carry such printed tomes to the table. These *destination wine outlets* still exist, as do their sommeliers with sterling silver tasse de vins dangling via tri-coleur ribbons around their necks.

This is devoted to the middle or upper-middle ground – restaurateurs who recognize the importance of wine to their outlet's revenue stream and who already appreciate the immense value that wine adds to their guests' mealtime enjoyment. With that, here's what we recommend:

- Be prepared to refresh your wine list regularly. Not only do vintage years change, but so too does the wine list that you will be selecting. Get used to it.
- Find two or three reliable suppliers or merchants and get to know them well. Rather than cruise the market, you are better off to create relationships with a few specialists. If you have a major operation, you may wish to expand the supplier list or even buy direct, but this is reserved for the big boys. You are a restaurateur or hotelier, so stick to what you know then let the wine merchants deal with their specialty.
- Think local first, then regional, then national. Every guest loves a local story and is prepared to scrutinize a plethora of local vintages. Providing that you are not purveying turpentine, local vineyards give you the opportunity to support your community and add novelty. As well, it's a two-way street; local vineyards you support will surely return the favor with a few well-placed referrals.
- Develop a mark-up strategy in line with your retail price points. Many restaurateurs use a sliding mark-up scale, reducing the percentage as the cost price increases. You should consider this and also the retail price points. Sticker shock for many customers will set in at the $50 threshold or perhaps $100 per bottle in premium

steakhouses and the like. This varies by region and typical guest. Learn about your customers and manage your lists accordingly.

- Developing your own private label wine can be a double-edged sword. We worked with one outlet whose own branded house wine (with a unique label that we designed) was so well priced and heavily purchased that it outsold most of the regular selections. A house wine for catering can make sense as a practical option. You might want to resist selling it in the dining room so that it will not deter from the full selection that you offer.

- Don't serve anything you wouldn't drink yourself. There's no room for anything that doesn't meet your own standards. Okay, we cannot have Chambertin or Latour every night, but surely even the most basic Pinot Noir can be excellent.

- Follow *Wine Spectator* and other leading journals. Look for up and coming wineries. Encourage dialogue with your wine merchants. Be prepared to test wines and take a chance with your inventories.

- Bin end sales work. Everyone loves a bargain. Having one or two bottles that are marketed as 'limited quantity' encourages the customer to purchase.

- Have a clearly defined by-the-glass program. While somewhat excessive, we have seen fine restaurants offering a dozen different wines by the glass, some at prices well beyond the realm of logic. We are still somewhat sticker-shocked by the $25+ per glass wines. The Coravin™ systems are examples of ways to have super premium bottles available by the glass. Moreover, there are recorking systems now offered that will allow you to extend the shelf life of part bottles for weeks versus hours.

- Wine is all about fun. Fun comes from a knowledgeable wait staff who can talk freely about your wines and understand pairings. Since the wine order usually starts the meal, a good relationship between you and your customer can be created right from the start of the meal.

- We need not mention that wine contains alcohol. Your pourers must recognize that patrons can get just as inebriated on a $25 Chateau Plonk as a $1,000 Chateau Latour. It's all a matter of budget. Safe Serve or Smart Serve programs must be adhered to, protecting your guests as well as your property. Training is critical and should be mandatory.

Serve Smartly

We would be remiss to write a text on generating more wine sales without devoting one section to the most serious issue of drinking and driving. The statistics are almost mind-numbing; every day, some 30+ lives are lost due to crashes caused by drunk driving. To reframe this in a less abstract way, in the time it takes a party of four to go through a bottle – say, roughly an hour – another person has died from an alcohol-related death.

Here in Ontario, Canada where we reside, the government has long recognized the importance of this issue and established Smart Serve Ontario in 1995. Their mandate is to support the industry and to ensure that responsible alcohol service is aligned with public safety for the good of our communities. Most municipalities, states or countries have similar programs.

We interviewed Richard Anderson, Smart Serve Ontario's executive director, to get more information on this province's program so that you have a better sense of what the law's broader intentions are. We've covered extensively about how best to operate in a revenue-maximizing capacity, but it's still critical to limit this risk that can both lead to sizeable damages and long-lasting reputational harm.

What's the process for waitstaff to be certified as Smart Servers?
We have made the process very simple. The program is online and those who are interested simply go to our website, register and take our course. It is easy to follow and requires a final examination. In Ontario, anyone who sells, serves, handles or delivers alcohol is required to be trained. We also recommend that restaurant, security and management be certified.

What is the risk of drinking and driving to the hotelier or restaurateur?
Duty of care is the main responsibility. That duty ensures that the patron is not overserved but furthermore gets home safely after. Anyone who serves a patron to the point of intoxication will accept liability should that

person be injured or that person injure someone else due to the intoxication caused by the overservice.

What is the best approach for a server when there is a group drinking so that a designated driver is identified?
A simple approach would be to ask. Many licensed operators provide free non-alcoholic beverages to the individual identified as the designated driver. But importantly, even with a designated driver, an establishment must ensure that no guest is served to the point of intoxication. Here in Ontario, the law states that the minute someone has been served to the point of intoxication, the liability is now assumed by the server and the individual holding the license to sell alcohol. For that reason, it is very important to monitor intake and the patrons' behaviors to ensure that they are always kept safe.

What should hoteliers and F&B operators do to protect their businesses?
You should be fully aware of the legal issues in your jurisdiction. And our recommendation is simply this: recognize the issue, train your staff and reinforce the importance of safe behaviour. Wine tasting should be fun and enjoyable. Let's all do our part to keep it that way.

Making Your Wine List Work for You

Wine can be a big source of revenue for your business. It can also be intimidating. Aside from price, confusion and lack of knowledge are two barriers to purchase. Luckily, both can easily be avoided with a comprehensive menu redesign. This chapter is more of a 'Wine 101' for those properties without a well-defined wine program already in place. If this comes off as overly simplistic – which is one of the key points of our argument, by the way – then chug ahead to subsequent pages where we discuss some more sophisticated wine strategies.

To begin, let's use the example of the *Yellow Tail* wine brand, as was wonderfully illustrated in the marketing theory book, "Blue Ocean Strategy" (2004). The parent company, Casella Wines, worked hard to diffuse any bewilderment surrounding wine purchases by making it very simple for those with limited experience to understand.

At their North American launch, Casella Wines started with only one red and one white varietal, and didn't bog down the labeling with complex grape names, obscure tastes or vineyard source locations. All the bottle had was the official name, *Yellow Tail*, and an illustration of a kangaroo – an animal wholly indicative of Australia and a clear marker for the brand. The flavors were always light, sweet and easy to get into. The bottle exudes fun.

We're not writing this for the supreme echelon of eateries, but rather the in-between, family style joints. Unless you operate a Michelin-star-winning, best-of-the-Zagat-guide, sommelier-employing restaurant, consider making your wine list more accommodating to those without a bachelor's degree in viticulture.

And by accommodating, what we're really suggesting is simplification. The last think you want is someone to stare slack-jawed at your wine list and mutter, "I don't know." Per the paradox of choice, the more options you give a person, the harder it is for them to make a selection, especially when they don't understand everything they're reading.

Most wine menus are sorted by white and red with subcategories for specific grapes or regions. The broad delineators of white and red work, but the subcategories often don't. Although it may come as a surprise for those inundated with F&B terminology, many people will not know the differences between a Sauvignon Blanc and a Pinot Grigio or a Cabernet Sauvignon and a Pinot Noir. Chardonnay? Shiraz? Burgundy? Bordeaux? Few actually know and, importantly, few have the time to bother learning.

Start by making it fun. Instead of organizing by varietal, sort by dominant flavors. For whites, think 'sweet', 'dry', 'fruity' or 'tart'. For reds, consider 'light', 'strong', 'spicy' or 'bold'. Not only are these categories easier to understand, but they will also inject the menu with excitement.

Next is brevity. A long list means more options – more choice, more trouble, more time spent deliberating and more time per dining cover. Work with your F&B director or chef to decide on a comprehensive menu that encompasses a full spectrum of tastes but is as lean as can be. See if you can fit it on one page in large type. How about half a page? What if you only had four whites and four reds? Would that make for an easy decision?

Third, don't clutter your wine list with too much information. Just as *Yellow Tail* never stressed the vineyard location, neither should you. Put the grape varietal and year of production in small type, then give an account of the dominant tastes, but keep these descriptors brief as well as alluring or action-oriented.

You will also want to emphasize local vintners if your location allows it. This is the one exception where we'd list the vineyard and winery. Out-of-towners and international customers will be curious to learn about the local produce. Take the time to educate them with perhaps a small blurb that highlights some unique aspects of the region.

Lastly, at the bottom or on a separate page, you can make it even easier by describing a selection of recommended wine pairings. Be sure to emphasize how each wine works to enhance and contrast the flavors of specific appetizers or mains. Then, naturally, use fun and moving descriptors to help nudge people in the right direction. Work with your restaurant manager or in-house wine buyer to plan a new wine menu that stresses how fun and effortless wines can be.

Developing Your Wine Strategy

Building a wine collection or contemplating any wine purchase is a huge cost and cannot be undertaken without adherence to an identified vision. The beverage must serve the role of generating profit at a revenue as well as the less quantifiable goal of heightening guest satisfaction – both patrons to a dining outlet and as a reason to stay at or return to a hotel containing said restaurant.

Hence, a solid wine strategy must define the parameters for how these beverages are positioned to meet certain objectives at the merchant or hotel level as well as for any governing brands or franchises. Here are some key considerations to craft a lucrative strategic plan:

Target Audience: The wine selection must be tailored to the customer depending on what markets the brand is hoping to develop inroads with. Often, the interests of those seeking leisure accommodations at a hotel, group event planners and other local, restaurant-only patrons do not align.

Catering: It's not uncommon to have two different wine lists. One may be built for singular, by-the-glass or varied bottle sales with reasonable markups, while the other is designed for the tonnage of weddings, reunions and corporate retreats. Different needs call for different arrangements with suppliers. As well, note that events are often booked many months in advance, so you need to be able to present wines that can be finalized 30 days out.

Theme: As many customers choose based on type of cuisine first, the wine must be congruent with the food the restaurant offers and not the other way around. Theme is not just about expectation management – for instance, people expecting a good glass of chianti at a low-key Italian joint – but about maximizing the experience and making memories. Beyond matching to the country, a fish restaurant will typically have more whites versus a steakhouse more reds, and then you must consider wine styles and grape varietals.

Local Influences: Hotels must show deference to the community, both for support and to help build a unique experience. Are there any wineries nearby and, significantly, are any of them worthy of more than a token local inclusion?

Pricing: You start with costs then broadly define a markup coefficient. From there you examine prices based on past sales and market psychology for variable markups. There should also be a standard process for regular reassessments to maximize sales versus profit per bottle. That is, maximizing per-bottle markup may reduce the total bottles sold and is therefore less efficient than a slight markup reduction to increase throughout. As it concerns premium selections, would you consider adding a limited quantity of high-priced bottles onto the list for special occasions like Champagne celebrations?

Private Labels: Would you consider stocking a house red and house white? If so, what's your price point and can you achieve a three-times markup? What are your cashflow requirements to guide order quantities?

Inventory: Storage costs and available space are important considerations as are revenue forecasts and turnover. Establish an appropriate dollar value for the total wine inventory along with a complete analysis of the number of labels housed. Part of this element is also the availability of supply in terms of working with reliable suppliers or wine merchants. Understand their terms and conditions, minimum order quantities and reordering speeds.

Wine List Presentation: What's the menu design? How many by-the-glass options are you including? How do you print your wine list and how easy is it to update? For example, guests don't like it when the stated vintage year is 2020 and the server appears with a 2021 bottle.

Cashflow: It's often said that the success of every business relies on this and the same is true for any alcohol where there's an upfront cost. Wine merchants are typically cash on delivery and you may need to purchase many more cases of wine to take advantage of better pricing or vintage availability. The rub is that these outflows don't usually coincide with peak hotel occupancy or other periods of high restaurant volume.

Your Wine List Sucks

Quite the chapter title, but, sadly, it is too often true. To address this more politely, think of this in terms of a few questions. What does your wine list stand for? Is it meaningful for customers? Does it fit with the theme and business plan for the parent restaurant?

Of course, we are talking about branding and marketing as much as we are talking about the physical alcohol inventory. While most of this critical exercise will be handled by the restaurant itself or the hotel's marketing department, the wine list must still match the greater vision if it is to shine and to sell.

For this, we've come up with the fun acronym of *CAMERA* so you can take a big 'picture' look at your beverage offerings with seven key guidelines to help you craft a menu that doesn't induce apathetic yawns or sneers.

Congruency: To repeat the obvious, all alcoholic offerings must fit with the restaurant's theme and its intended clientele. It must be a harmonious effort to tell a consistent narrative. For example, if you're opening a fancy, thousand-dollar-per-meal steakhouse, then, sure, stock a few bottles of Château Mouton Rothchild. But if you are running a bustling pizzeria designed for lots of covers and fast turnovers, you might consider only a few whites and reds to simplify the decision process so you can turn those tables even faster. We've even seen a swanky trattoria realize incredible success with only one house red for a buck an ounce.

Approachability: Is the wine list approachable to the average customer? Although not necessary the same as affordability, there is a significant overlap. While there will always be the high rollers and special occasion diners willing to splurge on expensive Champagne or a rarified Bordeaux, such individuals run contrary to current restaurant trends. The future of dining is one of reasonable pricing and sampling the unknown while still inviting patrons into an environment that's fun and enlightening. With the millennial cohort now acting as the guiding force for new concepts and openings, start to think about small batch, craft infusions, exciting glassware, tasting flights, wines with a story behind them and all without any egregious sticker stock.

Memorability: If you were to distill your restaurant's beverage offerings down to one single sentence, one phrase, one elevator pitch or one quintessential drink that will be the bell of the ball on social media for next five years, what would this be? Consumers nowadays are so bombarded with media and businesses vying for their attention that sometimes the only way to cut through all this noise is to simplify your concept down to its most emotionally titillating component. Once you find that, work to amplify it and complement it to round out the drinking experience.

Exceptionality: In a nutshell, if all you have in stock is what's also offered at the local liquor shop, then whoever built your wine list is just plain lazy. True, one can make the argument that what's familiar to guests is what makes it approachable and thereby increases sales, but we would argue strongly for the opposite point of view. If what you have on your beverage list is what's available at the convenience store down the street, then you're also giving your customers a direct price comparison to see just how much you're ripping them off. Instead, it is the unique twists and subtle differences in both the beverages themselves and their presentation to each guest that will earn you buzz, return visits and the ability to justify a higher price.

Regionality: As an offshoot of both memorability and thematic congruence, diners nowadays want to delve into the story of a specific geographic area. Even if only for that one meal experience, they want to immerse themselves in a culture, time and place, for which your wine list is but one element of the overall equation. For instance, a trend of late that we're big fans of has been the *hyper-regionalization* of European wines and restaurants. No longer can you simply open an Italian or French restaurant and hope to garner any level of sustained attention without an edge, like a Michelin chef, celebrity benefactor, opulent décor or some sizeable marketing oomph. Instead, people are opening Sicilian, Genovese, Provençal or Savoyard restaurants, with the beverage selections narrowcast on each respective territory's local produce and heritage.

Accessibility: Different from approachability, this pertains to the actual physical display for your list. The key is to enhance a patron's sense of discovery while also not inducing decision fatigue. You want your alcoholic listings to be a pleasure to read – that is, legible fonts with breathability on the page – but not too long so that it makes it difficult to come to a final selection within a reasonable timespan. It is as much an art as it is a science, and a job more suitable to a graphic designer. Still, though, you must ensure that the list only features the wines and other spirits that best represent your theme. Less is more. And if you have a long list, consider an abridged version accompanied by a binder or a tablet app for servers to hand out on request to true oenophiles.

Your Wine List Is Too Long

One of the fundamental marketing principles we abide by is: Keep It Simple Stupid. While that fourth word is often incorporated only to make it into a highly memorable acronym (KISS), it is not far from the truth because all of us, as lovers of wine, often unconsciously incorporate insider terminology or overestimate how much a customer cares about this trade knowledge. Assuming stupidity ensures that we don't overcomplicate or bewilder with expertise.

Perhaps the more apt word, though, is 'busy' in that your customers are all too rushed and distracted to notice everything that's happening around them, including the many nuances of crafting a great wine menu. For example, you stand at a busy urban intersection. Have you noted the make and model of every car that has passed by? Have you read every billboard? Do you notice the attention to detail that goes into each person's fashion sense? Our brains generate an overall impression of all these, but rarely do we drill down to specific details or remember anything shortly after the intersection is behind us.

We have so much on our minds that concentrating on any one particular thing for an extended period of time or even giving something the attention it deserves is impossible. In this sense, we are all indeed 'dumb' in one area of knowledge or another because there are so many worldly fascinations and so much beauty all around us that we fail to properly observe every day. Wine and other spirits exist in this harried, hectic ecosystem where most people have too many other ideas, tasks and pursuits vying for their precious time and beverage knowledge isn't a priority.

So, you're an idiot, and we're even bigger ones! Big whoop. To this day it amazes us that we're all still able to keep society functioning, let alone create marvels like cellphones and rocket ships. Thus, keeping your marketing message simple is of the utmost importance because if a customer must think about your offer – even for a moment – you've lost them; they have better things to do.

Keeping your wine list as succinct as possible gets to the heart of this marketing tenet because if you give your guests too many options, it can have dire consequences on the overall dining experience.

For starters, a longer wine list means more time spent deciding what glass or bottle to order. Even if this boils down to a matter of seconds, those seconds will amount to – especially if your restaurant is busy –fewer table turns per day and less alcohol ordered. Next, and related to this, placing the order will consume more of your servers' time. While this may be preferred in some instances to deepen the rapport with patrons, oftentimes it can delay the waiters from helping another table. Again, the seconds add up; an extra minute of wine list indecisiveness at 6pm could mean a 20-minute backlog by 7:30pm – that is, if you are running a popular spot.

Part of the reason why the contemporary wine list – and the entire drink menu for that matter – often becomes too long is that it tries to be everything for everyone. Another marketing mantra to deploy here is, "If you are good at everything, then you are great at nothing." Or, to reconcile it with the axiom in the opening sentence: Keep It *Specific* Stupid.

Often these extensive wine lists with generic offerings from around the world are the result of a wine merchant acting on behalf of those wineries or vendors who are willing to give them a few perks on the side for pushing certain brands. A common result here is a focused mess of a wine list with no overall unity to make it at all memorable to the guest. For instance, why do many American restaurants offer a full range of Australian Shiraz when they already have impeccable equivalents coming from their own backyard?

Our response to this is to give such acts of collusion the middle finger and focus on being as locally authentic or regionally specific as possible. As an example of the former, if you operate a hotel in Southern California, you might opt for a wide array of bottles from Santa Ynez and the Central Coast with only a token acknowledgement of Napa and Sonoma and nothing from anywhere else.

The latter is a bit different, insofar as it's not necessarily local, but it is paying tribute to the core theme of the restaurant. If you run an upscale Southern Italian eatery, you might opt for a list that only includes standard skews and private imports from Sicily, Calabria, Basilicata and Puglia, but with nothing from the northern mainstays of Abruzzo, Tuscany, Veneto or the Piedmont. Regional specificity also means knowing when to eschew your wines in favor of other culturally relevant beverages. For example, a casual Mexican restaurant would best let wine take a backseat to margaritas and cervesas with perhaps only a few tempranillos or other easy drinkers from the Latin world offered by the glass. (As an aside, Mexico is also starting to produce some good drops from the Baja California region.)

In this sense, the number of different labels and the types of wine you offer must relate directly back to the restaurant's *unique selling proposition* (USP). Be forewarned, though, if every bistro and eatery already had a high degree of confluence between the beverages and the dishes that are presented to customers, then we would have no reason to write this section.

The flip side to this argument for brevity pertains to those places at the very upper end of haute cuisine or those that are bona fide wine bars. Five-star dining establishments are well within the definition of special occasion and so the expectation is to take your time with what bottle to choose as well as to have a knowledgeable server or sommelier help you with your selection. For these sorts of eateries, an inventory consisting of hundreds of different bottles may be advantageous to help patrons feel like it truly is a special occasion.

And even then, simplicity in the wine list can help you to nudge customers into buying the more expensive offerings. You decide, but if you must take away one lesson from all this, it's that there's a reason why the KISS principle has stood the test of time and it isn't just that it's a catchy acronym.

Wine Is a Story About People

You drink wine. You have a fondness for white or red. You have your favorite producing countries, regions, varietals, blends, vineyards and wineries. Then you can also consider terroir, age of the vines, vintage, aging process and yearly climatic fluctuations. There's a reason why good sommeliers must go to school to perfect their expertise. Wine is a complex story with many layers to regale the novice to even the most veteran drinker.

Increasingly, though, it's becoming a story about people above all else. It doesn't matter about country of origin, the prestige of the winery, microclimate or specific grape planted; if the winemakers are knowledgeable and passionate then they will produce a fantastic drop.

The appellation closest to our hometown of Toronto – the Niagara Peninsula – offers an excellent example of this. Due to its geographical position of being between Lake Erie and Lake Ontario, and in combination with the buffering effects of a slightly inland escarpment, Niagara has long been known as an area fit for vinicultural activity. However, it was traditionally held suitable only for grapes meant for juice or, at best, jug wine varietals like Baco Noir.

Along came the 1970s and an emboldened generation of young winemakers who knew they could do better. Applying wisdom from the Old World and California, they slowly adjusted their practices to allow for more sophisticated production. This meant the careful grafting of international varietal vines, advanced crop rotations, the infusion of biodynamic techniques and deducing which grape was most appropriate for each specific hectare of land.

Five decades later, Niagara is still a relatively small growing region with most wines made for immediate consumption by an unrefined palate. And yet, there are Pinot Noirs that rival anything out of Burgundy or Oregon as well as a select few red blends far above everything from Bordeaux except for the first growths and grand crus. Furthermore, Niagara is world-renowned for its ice wines – whether it's a Vidal, Gewürztraminer, Kerner or Cabernet Franc, no other region even comes close.

One local label that we're particularly fond of is Stratus Vineyards and just because they roll out the red carpet every time we've visited! They are a niche producer, but they pay attention to nearly step in the winemaking process, from soil filtration and matching the right grapes with the right microclimate to the scrupulous design of the winery itself. It's one of the only LEED-certified (Leadership in Energy and Environmental Design) buildings of its kind, with precise geothermal temperature controls for the aging storehouse. Importantly, the practice of gravity flow is used for every cask, meaning that no pumps, oxygen and mechanical pressure are applied to the wines prior to bottling to ensure the best possible flavor.

Even though on paper, LEED and gravity flow features may seem like no-brainers, rest assured that they are each millions of dollars in extra overhead costs. To convince the financial backers as well as every new consumer of why these incremental details are essential, it requires people who are wildly passionate about wine. Without their commitment to perfection, undoubtedly Stratus would be making vastly different tastes than it does today.

And while we highlight this winery close to home, the same story is being played out across the globe. Australia was only a fledgling producer yet now its Shiraz is a wonder to behold. Ditto for Argentina and its Malbec or New Zealand and its Sauvignon Blanc. More recently, a case can be made for the German Rhineland, which was once only utilized for Müller-Thurgau or other table varieties but now makes exquisite Riesling, Spätburgunder and Dornfelder among others. Soon we will be writing a similar story about the maturation of the Croatian, Georgian, Lebanese, Hungarian and Romanian growers.

Above all else, and quite like any other aspect in hospitality, wine is a story about people. If you have the right people with the right craft, they will find a way to make a delicious libation, no matter the soil quality, climate, incumbent reputation or vine quality. Passionate winemakers will find a way.

Our Sober Curious Rebuttal

There's an emerging trend that is none-too-friendly to your restaurant's beverage sales. Encapsulated by buzz terms like 'dry January', 'sober curious' or 'mindful drinking', more people nowadays are abstaining from alcohol or are drinking less overall. Many factors are contributing to this, foremost being the inculcation of health-focused news explaining why alcohol isn't necessarily the best for your organs. The cultural narrative now favors moderation.

But another prominent reason, particularly for millennials and centennials, is that alcohol also isn't good for your wallet; it's expensive to drink while dining out, and young people have less disposable income than previous generations. Hitting a bit closer to home here in Canada, but nevertheless a current issue in many other advanced economies, the recreational legalization of marijuana has resulted in more people consuming this cheaper-per-gram alternate. As legalization progresses throughout the world – first for cannabis then perhaps psilocybin mushrooms – the same behavioral substitution may also come into play.

These elements aside, following a three-week tropical cruise over the holiday break, we decided to go a full month without a drop of wine, beer or any other spirit. This gave us some time to reflect upon the various ways that alcoholic beverages have permeated our daily lives and social interactions. Moreover, as consultants whose specific job is to strategically help optimize revenues, the top question throughout this process was: How do beverages sales stay afloat in an era of abstinence?

The answer is that when life gives you lemons, you create non-alcoholic lemonade with a lot of creative flavor additives. Any beverage you offer must be exciting and competitively priced and non-drinkers are still open to spending. While fewer people are drinking, there are still numerous others who are on the search for craft beers, private-label wine imports or imaginative cocktails. Just make sure that the price tag is on par with your territory, so you aren't hindering return visits.

Next, accept that this sober curious trend isn't one you can fight. Rather, you must embrace it by providing this cohort of guests with a selection of new age specialty beverages such as elaborate mocktails, botanically infused nonalcoholic elixirs, ginger-based sodas or high-end cold teas. The future is decidedly much more health-minded, so investigate your options for a wider variety of smoothies, vegetable juices, restorative spiced fruit shots or drinks with nootropic additives.

Third and finally comes an existential rebuttal to this emerging trend. Alcoholic beverages are not merely a form of inebriation; they are a celebration of human progress. Dating as far back as archaeology will allow, alcohol has been with us at every step of civilized history. When you imbibe, you are experiencing and honoring a morsel of our collective heritage as we emerged from our paleolithic ways.

This is a story worth telling and lauding at every possible juncture, be it through a more defined theme of your restaurant's wine list, fleshing out the story of individual vineyards, writing about the specific origins of each cocktail on the menu or through enhanced server training. Embellish what makes each alcoholic offering exceptional so that your customers will come to appreciate them just as you do.

Above all, while moderation is now mainstream, alcohol consumption has always been about quality over quantity, and there are still numerous opportunities to build beverage sales in the coming years even as mindful drinking increases in prominence.

You Can't Learn Wine in a Day

As with selling most other things, it certainly helps to be both well-informed and passionate about a given item to convince a customer to make a purchase. With wine, a specific challenge restaurateurs and servers face is getting patrons to opt for a more expensive glass or bottle because this takes confidence and proficient knowledge in the subject matter. And one cannot become conversant in a day, meaning that continuous education – or in certain instances, a continuous professional development (CPD) program – is necessary to increase alcohol sales.

Before getting into some tactics, let's address why this is important now. First, as with everything, one long tail effect of the COVID-19 pandemic may be, for some, a lingering aversion to dining out, meaning fewer covers overall and in turn a necessary quest for driving more revenues on a per-table basis.

Related to this, the pandemic has hit many people in terms of diminished real wages or worse, thereby leading to tighter spending when out and a preference for the cheapest option if wine is the beverage of choice. The third reason is a bit more existential in that wine is gradually losing its prestige amongst younger drinkers who increasingly opt for zero-calorie hard seltzers, craft beer, cocktails or abstinence.

Taken together, it's not too farfetched to envision a scenario where only the least expensive inventory moves. Without enthusiastic servers to tell wine's multifarious story and guide customers towards the best pairing, revenues will be compromised as will meal satisfaction.

Specific to hotels, there's a halo effect here as any disappointment with the restaurant can emotionally transfer back to one's appreciation of the guestroom – that is, the totality of the onsite experience that is conveyed in an online review. Furthering this, in the pursuit of a more contactless guest journey, many hotels are deepening the consolidation of dine-in restaurant and delivery or room service operations, meaning that there's an opportunity for oenophilic guest service agents to upsell those guests wanting something sent to the suite.

Returning to the title, learning about wine is as much fun as drinking it (well, almost), and you increase your proficiency one glass at a time. This fits perfectly within the contemporary bite-sized learning or microlearning model whereby fifteen minutes per day results in far better information retention then sitting through an intensive, two-hour session once per week.

There's also a symbiotic relationship between education and passion. The more one is taught, the higher the likelihood that an individual will develop an innate curiosity for the subject matter. It's a bit of a virtuous circle in that regard, although teaching should be focused exclusively on quality over quantity of alcohol consumed. Here are some ideas to help round out your team's wine knowledge that they can sell it better and increase beverage revenues:

- Host team tastings both to build internal bonds and show your appreciation.
- Invite veteran servers, and not just sommeliers, restaurant managers or F&B directors, to attend meetings with wine merchants.
- Incorporate some tidbits of news on the latest inventory arrivals in the company bulletin board or internal newsletter.
- Post little factoids around the kitchen or embedded in emails to enhance microlearning.
- Announce news of any menu changes and new additions with simple notes that can be consumed in two minutes or less.
- Host team contests where the prize is a bottle or two of leftover inventory you are planning to sunset, with the aim of raising the team's appreciation for wine.

For many, the pandemic was a time for introspection, acquiring new skills and filling the void of social events with learning of all types. But the learning shouldn't stop now that we're all back out and about. Learning is a constant pursuit and to get your team into the routine of learning about wine, it must be codified as part of the operational process.

WINEMAKING
AND VARIETALS

The Importance of Vintage

"A 2008 Merlot? Or how about the 2009? Who cares about the year, just give us the one that tastes the best!" This may be a conversation you've overheard at a restaurant. It may have even been you uttering these words at one point. Or, instead of asking for the best of multiple options, you've simply demanded the cheapest. Importantly, ask yourself how many times multiple vintage years of the same product have appeared on your wine list.

Unless a patron has previously visited a specific winery and participated in a vertical tasting of different vintages from the same vines, he or she probably won't know very much about the nuanced aesthetic divergences from the same wine sampled year-over-year. Probably the three biggest components of a purchase are price, varietal and where the grapes were sourced. Vintage year doesn't really enter the equation. After all, this is bridging on the insider knowledge of sommeliers, and they probably wouldn't want to divulge too much of their expert wisdom lest they become obsolete.

And so, the question arises: is a vintage's specific year important to the average consumer? Perhaps not now it isn't. But therein lies an opportunity for you, the avid hotelier. The whole point of this book is to enlighten you on various topics concerning wine, whiskey, beer, cheese and anything else in-between so that you can pass the lesson along to your servers and they in turn can use said knowledge in conversations with patrons.

It's all about developing rapport and giving guests value. One way of accomplishing this is by being a proficient beverage guide to help patrons maximize the enjoyment of their meal.

Let's try this again: does vintage year *really* matter? Yes, because it is one more piece of the puzzle that your team should know so that they can enrich dining experiences and possibly sell some booze in the process. The year, by its very nature, also tells the consumer whether the wine is sufficiently bottle-aged and ready for consumption.

Before the mass adoption of complex, computer-controlled drip irrigation systems, vintage used to be far more important than it is today. That's because adverse weather could lead to underdeveloped grapes and low sugar volumes for the yeast to feed upon during fermentation. But this problem is quite manageable nowadays, even with El Niño, La Niña and whatever other manmade climate changes come our way.

Year-over-year weather conditions for behemoth production regions like California and the Mediterranean have many mechanisms in place to ensure stability of production, so the wines are also quite unwavering in their quality levels. Given that we live in Ontario, Canada, where we experience the full force of the four seasons, a farmer's almanac is a good resource to accompany any talk of vintage year. Because the growing season in our local viticultural region, Niagara-on-the-Lake, is effectively May through mid-September, the best years are ones with heavy storms in the beginning of the summer with a very hot, very dry August to help the grape skins thicken and concentrate sugars underneath. If we get a wet August, we get wines with lower acidity, reduced tannins and less of a sugar hit on the palate.

But this only really applies to one of the most northern (and minor from an overall volume of production standpoint) wine regions in the world. Consider how vintage applies to Australia, for instance, a continent where extremely low precipitation, almost drought-like conditions are prevalent.

Many doubt that vintage year is even worth discussing at this point due to our technological prowess, but we argue that it is still an element of the equation that patrons wouldn't mind knowing a bit about, especially at the ultra-upper end of the wine buying spectrum. In fact, vintage has such a strong legacy that you can buy wine futures, betting on how the wine will turn out based on the growing season's weather patterns. Little morsels of knowledge like this are all you need to add some life to the conversation and generate better rapport with guests.

Aging Barrels

When discussing wine and what differentiates one bottle from another, we've already touched on the three most common influencers – grape varietal, place of origin (country, appellation, terroir) and vintage. From a sales perspective, having confidence in your knowledge of these three will go a long way towards developing a 'wine story' to woo and sell to patrons. Just in case those three can't seal the deal, aging barrels represent a fourth element you can add to this conversation. In-barrel fermentation is also done but that's a separate topic from aging.

Aging wine in wood barrels can drastically alter the taste profile and often makes the beverage unrecognizable to its un-aged or steel cask counterpart. Discussing a label in terms of its unique aging process (or by talking about this in process terms) is a great way to deepen the story and guest-staff rapport, especially given that the effects of barreling aren't common knowledge. Such a chat may or may not lead directly to increased liquor sales on the spot, but it will most certainly augment the overall dining experience. Hence, everyone in the restaurant game should know a bit about how wine is aged.

At its most fundamental level, the only three materials for barreling you need to know are stainless steel, American oak and French oak. Stainless steel is the simplest, imparting minimal flavor and allowing the liquid to stew in its chemicals. The other two, however, are slightly porous, allowing for slow evaporation (concentration of flavor and aroma profiles) and oxygenation (softening the taste of the astringent tannins). Oak is exceptional in this porous-yet-watertight characteristic, making it the ideal wood for years-long wine maturation.

Next of importance is how much the coopers 'toast' the barrels – that is, how much they burn or char the insides. This is done to help shape the wood but more so to impart flavor to the wine as the reactive liquid slowly chews away at its inner lining over months or years and incorporates chemicals from the burnt oak into its flavor profile. A good barrel can withstand about three years of leaching from wine before it is rendered inert.

Of course, the flavors of toasted American and French oak differ greatly, with the former considered to impart bolder, more intense flavors and the latter often likened to sweeter tasting notes. Think butter, caramel, cinnamon and vanilla additions for whites and coffee, smoke and spice for reds. As barrels can impart stronger flavors, this becomes an issue when dealing with patrons who prefer mellow, sweeter wines. In these cases, a steel cask Sauvignon Blanc is better than a two-year, American oak Chardonnay, while a Pinot Noir would obviously be preferable to a Bordeaux aged in French oak.

As a restaurant manager or sommelier who has long understood the wooden aging process and its effects, the use of American oak, French oak or steel is likely second nature to you. However, if your palate is underdeveloped as is the case for newer servers, the best way to learn to distinguish these discrepancies is to complete a vertical tasting of the same wine matured under the three different conditions (steel, American oak and French oak).

And in terms of conveying this knowledge to the customer, it may be best to give your servers a quick elevator pitch on how aging barrels can let a freshly fermented wine evolve into something else entirely. This slow process is somewhat magical in its own right and will definitely add to the narrative to help the sale.

More recently, we've also seen a few esoteric barrel profiles added to the aging mix, often as marketing tools for middling wines sold at the low to mid-price range in stores. Foremost among these would be aging in Bourbon barrels, imparting sharp, smoky hints of the sour mash to the final product. While many of these are more gimmick than gem, the marketing differentiator can be wielded nevertheless.

Focusing on Terroir

While the average drinker will focus on the grape varietal, the vintage and the country of origin (including that region's established growing practices), they seldom direct their attention to the combination of specific geography and geology as well as the resultant microclimates which help bestow each region's soil with unique properties that are ultimately expressed in the grapes.

The word that best describes this topographical consideration is *terroir*, and its mere mention makes for a good talking point with patrons.

Many people know the word in passing because of its alluring sound as it rolls off the back of the throat. Others won't be familiar with or have even heard of terroir, so it's up to your waitstaff to educate guests (if prompted) in as simple a manner as possible. Who doesn't like to learn something new after all?

Terroir will flesh out a bottle's story in an entertaining way and thereby enrich the overall dining experience. By knowing one or two facts about each vineyard's unique geological backstory, it will give servers yet one more angle to not only enhance liquor sales, but also to deepen the rapport with patrons.

For instance, suppose a guest is undecided between two bottles of red – the first is an outstanding, reasonably expensive Californian Zinfandel and the second is the cheapest one on the menu. Obviously, you should push for the upsell but, more importantly, because you know that this customer will enjoy the former selection. The question is: how do you go about convincing this patron to dish out the extra cash?

The best route is to extol the benefits of choosing the Californian through an emotional narrative. A brief description like this might touch on the unique flavor of this varietal, the vintage if it is noteworthy, perhaps a couple specific aspects of the winemaker's growing practices and the wine's terroir. For this fourth element, you might describe how the vineyard is situated along the leeward slope of a sierra which makes the microclimate just a touch drier that its neighbors and therein better concentrates the sugars in the grapes for a finer finish.

Discussions of terroir can incorporate proximity to mountain ranges like this along with closeness to rivers, headwaters, valleys, dormant or extinct volcanoes, mineral deposits, old growth forests or strong ocean currents. Terroir is blanket term for nearly everything that has or will affect the soil in which the grape roots will feed. And indeed, just about everything does affect how the fruit matures.

It isn't vital that your team know every characteristic of a bottle's terroir, but one or two interesting or exceptional aspects (told in a simplified manner) will go a long way towards enriching the stories used to sell more wine and boost the positive sentiments that consumers have for your restaurants.

What About Body and Structure?

A problem arises when we attempt to sell to these wine neophytes by using jargon that they may not fully comprehend. The response to the innocent question, "What's that wine like?" will often prompt the server or somm to blab on about that label, injecting some words about a good structure, being medium-bodied or some hybrid of those two descriptors. But do guests know what the terms 'body' and 'structure' mean? More significantly, do they even care?

In short, body defines the weight of a particular wine – how full you feel after consuming a healthy dose. On the other hand, structure is used to elaborate upon the overall quality and intricate union of all the assorted chemicals that encompass a certain wine. For instance, you might hear of a specific vintage being called out for being 'well-balanced' or having 'a good structure for aging'.

While both terms are great to know for general knowledge or a biochemical analysis and for your servers to build rapport with those patrons who already have a vinicultural acumen, the best course is to always keep it simple. When you introduce complex terminology that the listener must think about to process, you are in fact promoting this recipient to use more of their logical brain instead of allowing the emotional nerve centers to spark. Even the word 'astringent' is seldom understood as a heuristic for a tannin's mouth-drying effect.

As any good salesperson will tell you, people buy based on the latter (emotions), no matter how much they back-rationalize their decisions (logic). Hence, instead of deploying a cerebral lexicon while describing a wine, if you want the sale, it would be better to use modifiers that evoke the senses or elicit a vivid picture in one's mind, which in turn help to bring about an emotional reaction.

All too often, a server or sommelier will attempt to sell a specific vintage by throwing in phrases containing heady words like body, structure, tannins or astringency, and you can see the patron's eyes glaze over. Particularly while trying to impress a date, no customer will halt the sale to ask what one of these terms means. They'll just nod to save face. The results of not speaking the customer's language in this regard can range from them not taking the bait in trying the more expensive suggestion to not purchasing any alcohol whatsoever.

A good way to avoid this problem and to thus help boost revenues is to reeducate your team to steer clear of technical terms off the top and to memorize some adjectives that stimulate the senses of taste, smell, sight and touch. Below is a short list to get you started. And for reference, touch in the context of beverages is used to denote texture or 'mouth feel' as well as how the wine sits in one's stomach, and this sense is what's most often associated with 'body'.

Taste: fresh, sweet, mellow, rich, savory, subtle, bold, smooth, creamy, buttery, oaky, tangy, juicy, jammy (fruit-forward), citrusy, lemony, peachy, zesty, acidic, tart, earthy, spicy, nutty, peppery, chocolaty, bitter, smoky and hopefully not skunky

Smell: fragrant, aromatic, floral, fruity, plummy, herbacious, grassy, leafy, smoky, earthy, musky and woodsy

Sight: light, pale, bright, golden, green, emerald, amber, orange, dark, violet, pink, cherry red, ruby, brick, brown, thick and cloudy

Touch: vibrant, lively, playful, delicate, intense, light, silky, velvety, leathery, chalky, dry, heavy, hearty, dense, viscous, oily, complex and bubbly or fizzy (of course, if you are discussing any type of sparkling wine)

Obviously, there is some overlap for many of these words insofar as what sense they can be used for, and this is far from an exhaustive list. The overall point should be clear, though. Words that provoke a visceral response may help you far more than launching into a diatribe about the various constituents of a grape blend and how each minor component helps to lend more body or add structure to the wine. Feel free to get quirky with your adjectives or invent a word to make the description even more memorable.

Sometimes people don't care about our enthusiasm for wine's numerous intricacies and the story behind what makes a particular bottle noteworthy; sometimes they just want a quick glass that fits their moods. Read the room and don't complicate the sales process unless invited to do so, or you end up with less than you bargained for.

Organic Wines

Everybody is going organic these days – fruits, vegetables, meats, grains and now alcoholic beverages (and that's only including food products). The trend makes sense, too; people are concerned about what chemicals are being added to foods and how they affect their health. As it turns, many of these pesticides, herbicides, additives or genetically modified foods aren't great for you long-term, and hence 'going organic' nullifies many of these potential concerns. In terms of psychographics, the three basic mindsets of customers to consider are:

Devoted: Those whose diets are mostly or completely organic food and who go out of their way to uphold their nutritional beliefs.

Dabbling: Those who understand the benefits of eating organics and will purchase such foods when presented the opportunity but aren't strict about adhering to any restrictions. Think 'flexitarian' but for organic foods and not just animal products.

Disinterested: Those who don't care either way and might even be turned off by the extra markups associated with organic foods.

For people in the 'devoted' category, placing an organic white and an organic red on the menu is a big value-add. They shouldn't have to break their strict dietary regimens for you to sell them something. On the other hand, this group is small, albeit growing, and quite niche, so you shouldn't worry about building an entire organic wine list to appease these people. One white and one red will suffice; use accepted international grape varietals like Sauvignon Blanc and Merlot. Try to kill two birds with one stone by sourcing locally.

Contrarily, those in the 'disinterested' category probably won't be insulted by the existence of an organic wine on the menu, but they won't gravitate to this bottle or see this modifier as significant. For people in this camp – the present-day majority – the going belief is that while efforts in organic winemaking are commendable, on average the prestige and the overall flavor aren't yet up to snuff with established wineries.

This is the biggest hurdle for sales and in turn keeping organic bottles stocked. Devotees won't bring you enough revenues on this front because they are too few. And the brief conversation your server has with disinterested patrons shouldn't be dedicated to convincing them to change their minds. It's the middle ground that's the battleground – the dabblers.

As previously mentioned, this is the group that recognizes the organic food movement but won't commit itself to strict observance of the rules likely because it's logistically (and monetarily) impossible. The dabblers have quite the range, from those who are sometimes organic eaters to those who only partake occasionally but still keep an open mind to the underlying significance of it all. They might opt for an organic bottle with minimal cajoling or at least admire your efforts.

The best way to sell to dabblers or the disinterested is on the health factor – no chemicals or preservatives and made with better quality sugars (because of the differences in viticultural processes). You also must dispel the underlying skepticism that these wines aren't as flavorful or complex as other labels in the same price range. These rumors are baseless as organic winemaking has been perfected for several decades now.

As talking points, here are some other tidbits you might want to know. Organic wines are often touted as 'sulfur free'. Sulfites are an important additive for stabilization during the aging process as well as a major cause of wine headaches, and thus most organic wines are destined for young consumption (within three years). Next, while certain countries have organic certifications in place, many vineyards and wineries already abide by most of these standards but choose not to go through with obtaining official status because of the marginal costs associated with going that extra (and seemingly unnecessary) mile.

The bottom line: one white, one red is all you need for now, but feel free to add more if the demand is there. When the organic trend gains more ground than you should consider expanding this part of the wine list. For some restaurants that have branded themselves as wholly organic down to every last ingredient, it is only natural that this branding extends to the wine list.

Biodynamic Wines

As a sequel of sorts to an organic labeling, *biodynamic* takes this to the nth level with soil, plant and livestock health all considered ecologically interlinked. And the numbers reflect the obscurity of this practice as there are currently under a thousand wine producers worldwide following true biodynamic practices.

It all revolves around what is best for the health of the soil, especially during the off months when the grapevines are hibernating. Key principles include diverse crop rotations, a lack of herbicides or pesticides, the use of cover crops and the cultivation of green manures to enrich mineral content and carbon fixation. There's also a spiritual undercurrent to biodynamic agriculture whereby certain protocols dictate that ground quartz be dispersed over the terrain and stuffed animal horns be buried under the earth.

While appealing to a customer's desire for sustainable practices is a good angle, its effects will be muted because a vineyard's overall health is not a primarily reason to buy wine. The leading question is: does the wine taste great? And the answer for biodynamic labels is increasingly affirmative in this regard, both from blind taste tests and from both of our own personal experiences.

Ultimately, though, writing in the word 'biodynamic' on the menu is nothing more than a conversation starter and a modifier to induce more sales. While the latter point is quite straightforward, it's the former one that interests us more. If a patron asks what is implied by biodynamic, this is a greenlight for the server or bartender to launch into a concise story and, importantly, to build rapport with said guest.

Meal satisfaction is more than just the food on the plate; it's the furnishings, the sounds, the service, the crowds and the personal relationships formed with staff. A running current throughout this book is to educate your team and make sure that they are passionate about wine, so that they can boost alcohol sales and add another dimension to the dining experience. And given the correlation between how a guest feels about their meal and their overall satisfaction with your outlet, it goes without saying that augmenting the dining experience should be a consummate goal. Adding organic and biodynamic wines gives customers one more point to spike the memorability of the experience.

Dessert and Ice Wines

Although not nearly as prestigious as other growing regions in California or France, the Niagara Peninsula close to our hometown of Toronto is recognized as a world leader when it comes to ice wines – a subcategory of dessert wines where the producers don't pick the grapes until after the first frost hits the vines.

When we last visited the winemaker Stratus Vineyards in

Niagara-on-the-Lake for a tasting, we were awed by their use of such sweet wines. No longer just an accompaniment to a chocolate mousse or crème brûlée, their ice wines were served with cheeses. The unbridled sweetness of a Riesling ice wine matched swimmingly with piquant cheddar; a fruity Vidal ice wine paired with mellow gouda; the complex red berry tastes of a Cabernet Franc ice wine contrasted perfectly with a sharp, salty blue stilton. All exquisite.

The takeaway for you is that dessert wines aren't solely for dessert, nor are they solely for cheeses. What about pairing such sweet wines by the glass with appetizers? Think lobster bisque and Sauternes. On a recent trip to the Fairmont Le Manoir Richelieu in the Charlevoix Region of Quebec, Canada, we sampled an apple cider ice wine with foie gras – a surprisingly playful combination.

Dessert wines have a rich history. There is a wide variety, and while Canada is known for its ice wine, many other regions produce their own local gems – German Eiswein and Trockenbeerenauslese, Austrian Ausbruch, French Sauternes and Hungarian Tokaji to name a few. Sweet wines are often underappreciated. Incorporating them into your menu is an excellent opportunity for added revenue.

The key to selling sweet wines outside of their predefined after-dinner utility is to offer them by the glass. For most of your customers, dessert or sweet wines aren't nearly as familiar as their red and white cousins. For others, they're just too sweet to consume at any significant quantity. Even though bottle sizes are often only 200mL or 375mL, it's still a hefty commitment, especially given that dessert wines edge on the expensive side. Offering sweet wine by the glass eliminates these obstacles. People will be more adventurous with a one-ounce portion – a suggested serving size that's adequate for a taste and keeps selling prices reasonable while still maintaining your margins.

Start by reviewing with your chef and restaurant manager what sweet wines you currently stock and how a few common varietals might be matched with your selection of appetizers. Next, consider putting a cheese plate on the menu with suggested pairings. Better yet, how about a flight of dessert wines to give patrons a more formal introduction and make for a highly experiential meal component. Last, educate your staff so that they can properly communicate how great these wines taste and how well they complement certain foods.

Rosé for Summer

Everyone knows what rosé wine looks like and that it's great for summer dining. Beyond matching the name and the season, the rest is an enigma. If your customers have a little more insight about rosé, perhaps they'll consider it beyond only those hot summer alfresco occasions, and you'll soon find yourself out of stock!

The first myth to bust is that rosé (also rosato in Italian and rosado in Spanish) is not a blend of white-skinned and dark-skinned varietals, at least not real rosé. Instead, think of it as an incomplete red. The grapes are crushed and allowed to soak for a few days, but then the skins are drained away from the juice, as opposed to being fully macerated then left in for the fermentation leg of the process. Typically, the amplitude of rosé's orange-pink coloration is determined by how long the skins are left in contact with the juice prior to pressing.

As a side note, one rarer form of rosé – the Vin Gris – is the result of immediately pressing the grapes with no time allowed for maceration (that is, the soaking or leaching of pigments from the skins into the juice). Vin Gris is a hard find, partly because of low awareness (lack of demand) but also because the process doesn't allow for a high yield (less revenue). If you ever stumble upon one, give it a try; the pale amber-pink and subtle cherry-melon tastes are impeccable.

In general, rosé has a vibrant rouge color with a range of fruity flavors but far less of a sugary spike like that of whites. Part of what makes rosé so well equipped for summer, and especially alfresco dining, is the way such wines pair with seasonal dishes. These light reds can work with nearly any type of poultry, fowl or fish main as well as sides of bitter greens, sweet carbs, creamy pastas or succulent fruit. The dry acidic taste of this beverage will never dominate or obfuscate a dish. In short, they are very food-friendly and extraordinarily flexible in application. That, and they are served chilled to offset a hot, humid day.

The largest producer of rosé also happens to be a part of the world with the quintessentially ideal summer – Provence. This is where the technique was honed, and it is where you'll source the best. But also keep your tongue alert for interesting batches from Spain, Italy, South Africa, South America and, of course, California. We've always found that the traditionally hearty deep, full-bodied grapes do not make for the best rosé. We normally adhere to Pinot Noir, Grenache, Gamay, Syrah and other soft reds that can make for a dry rosé.

If you're finding that rosé is a tough sell as a table wine for the course of a meal, consider positioning it as a starter wine – as a sangria-esque alternative to an opening round of drinks prior to appetizers or entrées. Such a by-the-glass approach may cannibalize the higher-markup cocktails, but these concoctions have a far larger labor component over a straight pour. These 'light reds' can also be introduced as a more sophisticated substitute for white wine. Any way you go about it, when summer shines, rosé should be top of mind for your staff and your guests.

Trio de Pinot

Ahh, Pinot, a perennial favorite. And not because we're hopping on the *Sideways*, it's-so-temperamental-so-you-have-to-love-it bandwagon, but because we love the light, fruity taste, and its translucent, crimson-violet color. Plus, it can pair with just about any main, be it meat, chicken, fish, veggie or cheese.

Most of our gratitude applies to Pinot Noir – the red or dark, purple-skinned grape of the family – but the other two key siblings are also worth trumpeting. These two are Pinot Gris (or Pinot Grigio if you find yourself in Italy) and Pinot Blanc. As colors are the going descriptors for the Pinot grape, Gris implies gray or opaque pinkish-brown skins while Blanc denotes white or pale-yellow varietals.

This trio of Pinot represents quite a diverse collection of wines both Old and New World. For starters, the 'Pinot' stems from the French for 'pine', so called because the grapes bundle in such a way as to look like pinecones. Next, Pinot wines get their clear hues from the slenderness of the fruit's skins as well as the skin's anthocyanin (a powerful antioxidant) and polyphenol concentration. Their thin-skinned and tight-packed nature is what makes them more prone to rot and disease over other grapes (hence, temperamental).

If the French in the name is any hint, the Pinot family originates in France, specifically the treasured growing region of Burgundy where it has been cultivated since Roman times. Fast forward to the modern era and Pinot Noir is one of the *international grapes*, finding homes in vineyards from Italy and Germany (where it is named after its source region – Frühburgunder and Spätburgunder) to New Zealand, California, Oregon and just outside of our hometown of Toronto in Niagara-on-the-Lake, Ontario.

Through decades of experimentation (that is, drinking), the two of us have grown particularly fond of the Burgundy and Californian expressions. The former uses Pinot Noir almost exclusively for its red wine production – with the most prestigious ones denominated as grand crus – while a few degrees north this dark grape is blended in as a key contributor to Champagne. Then a few degrees east – in Alsace – the Pinot Gris and Pinot Blanc are crowning achievements. On the Pacific Coast, the famous Napa and Sonoma Valleys as well as the Central Coast make good use of Pinot Noir and Pinot Gris, both possessing a quintessential New World taste.

Interestingly, all Pinot grapes are sub-varietals of the same species. Although nowadays the growing and grafting is a rigorously controlled process, mutations of the skin have resulted in many obscure pedigrees like Pinot Rouge, Pinot Meunier, Pinot Moure and Pinot Teinturier. Together, whether it's a red or a white, a Pinot drop will be light bodied with heavy tastes and aromas of fruit (red berries in the case of reds, spicy tropical fruit for whites).

This gives them versatility, but it also opens the doors to some rather peculiar pairings. Pinot Noir can match with light red meals like snapper, chicken parmesan, veal medallions or just about anything using tomato sauce as a base. Due to the spicy, smoky flavor of Pinot Gris, in addition to its darker-than-usual, golden-copper color, it is primed for some bizarre pairings where you'd typically advocate a red – roasted pork, turkey, lean meats like venison and dishes with mushroom-based sauces. Pinot Blanc is the odd one out of the three and it could be added to the menu exclusively for that purpose. It's a very soft drop missing the strong acidity of other whites, making it suitable for salads, creamy pastas or flaky white fish.

Baco the Other Noir

For fans of Old World flights and all other types of wine purists, a fledgling North American hybrid varietal is probably not top of mind. Even though putting the spotlight on Baco Noir affords us the chance to boast about yet another form of vinicultural innovation happening in here in Ontario and the state of New York, that's hardly enough to warrant the rest of the globe's attention.

Rather, a short anecdote about Baco Noir that we fondly remember demonstrates two critical factors when selling wine at a restaurant. While hosting a dinner party, a friend with very limited wine knowledge brought over a bottle of what he gleefully touted as a 'Black Bacon Wine' that came recommended by the stock clerk at the local liquor store. As a Canadian (a bilingual country), he should have known that 'Baco' is not the word for bacon in French, although we can see why he was deceived as a direct translation is 'le bacon' and he did get the 'Noir' part right.

In any case, once the novelty of a lardon-flavored wine was debunked, he begrudgingly responded with something quite profound. "Well, I only really know Cabernet Sauvignon, Merlot and Chardonnay. I guess I'll should just stick to what I know."

Unpacking the sentiment in this declaration reveals two generic observations about your customers. And these two lessons pertain not only to your liquor sales, but they also have applications for your entire slate as well as how you position all other facets of your operation.

First is that a sizeable chunk of the population probably does not know a whole lot about wine nor are they passionate about upleveling their knowledge base. If you overestimate their basal level of interest then you risk alienating a customer. People don't dine out for a lecture series; they want to be entertained; getting too academic risks losing an upsell on a more expensive bottle or the sale itself. Moreover, feeding patrons with too many choices all at once may result in someone who was about to purchase an entire bottle reverting to a by-the-glass order, therein spending far less overall.

Secondly, you must always fall back upon the mantra of giving your customers exactly what they want. Despite what the average person thinks about his or her own sense of adventurism, sometimes we are all traditionalists by craving what we already know. This is the psychological thrust behind comfort foods. After a long day in the office or dealing with stressors like airport-to-airport travel, often we just want a taste of the familiar to fade our lambent minds. While we are all likely guilty in one way or another of attempting to transform our wine lists into a shelter for the erudite oenophile, such wild exploration left unchecked may in fact turn off some guests who are only in the mood for a jug of inexpensive, smooth Malbec.

How you invite guests into the vast and verdure world of wine without simultaneously rendering it unapproachable to neophytes? As before, keep it simple. By limiting choice, you prevent the onset of decision fatigue. Next, always leave one or two *staple options* on the menu for the intractable novices, then print them close to the top for easy readability. Third is a slight retraining of your team, whereby they must learn to express their wine knowledge through a digestible narrative and not through industry jargon.

Now as for the varietal itself, Baco Noir is an aromatic, woodsy-yet-fruity and slightly smoky dark red. It was named after Francois Baco who successfully hybridized it during the turn of the century in response to the phylloxera blight that had just swept through Europe. As a cross between the European *Vitis vinifera* and the North American *Vitis riparia* strains, it was resistant to the fungus but still no match for the former vines in terms of prestige and complexity.

Today, Baco Noir is more commonly planted in burgeoning production regions throughout the Northeast where it is perfectly suited to the harsher American and Canadian climates. Due to its rustic qualities, it pairs nicely with any grilled or barbecued meats, although it is still largely a *food wine* in terms of flavor intricacy. On any given night out, though, Baco Noir makes for a perfectly satisfactory and reasonably affordable drop. It's worth a try to see if it might fit on your wine list; just don't expect any mind-blowing tasting notes and certainly not any hints of bacon.

Low Cal, Low Carb Wines

The world of dining is becoming increasingly health-conscious, diet-focused, and phobic of calories, carbohydrates, trans-fats, gluten and a slew of other buzzed-about food components. Given this trend, it's no surprise that the beverage industry has responded in kind. People want to have their cake and eat it too – imbibing without the bloat of excess calories or other chemicals besides alcohol for the body to process.

For many years, the beer market has offered an exceptionally wide array of carbohydrate-reduced products. These are generally marketed as a 'light' product at only a slight compromise to ABV. According to an Allied Market Research study from 2021, light beer still only represents under 1% of the total suds market.

More recently, hard seltzers have captured the narrative, as epitomized by the fervor over deftly advertised brands like White Claw with international mainstays like Bud Light launching their own competitive products to keep customers in their domain. The broad success of these brands hinges on bringing together carbonated fruity flavors with very low sugar and calorie content, and most are also gluten-free.

Thus, it should come as no surprise that the wine industry is pivoting to capitalize on this new zeitgeist. Importantly, wine consumption in North America currently skews 59% female and 41% male; this also supports the introduction of more calorie-conscious and low-sugar products that can be implicitly marketed as 'slimming'.

Key throughout is to offer a wine alternative for the younger generations who are in general more aware of their daily carbohydrate intakes as a part of living a healthier lifestyle. Fair representation through the introduction of one red and one white offering that can be promoted as 'one gram of sugar per ounce' or via another simple phrasing will help to appease this cohort and not alienate them from starting to develop an appreciation of wine in their youth.

Our recommendation is to start with BTG offerings, for which most low-sugar wines are already targeted for this purpose by being relatively cheap and having twist-off tops in lieu of corks. Save your cellar space for more sophisticated vintages. While taste remains a top criterion for any procurement, recognize that the low-calorie options you ask your wholesaler about will be of middling quality (as sugars are often a key driver of flavor) and therefore cannot be priced above this context.

Mulled Wine and Other Holiday Spirits

Thinking December? 'Tis the season to be jolly, and there's no better way to help put you in a very merry mood than with a holiday-themed libation.

There's something about this time of year that brings out our indulgent side. It starts with that extra slice of pumpkin pie at Thanksgiving, and then it's a slippery slope all the way to through to the inevitable reckoning on New Year's Day and all the various proclamations of austere diets that only last for roughly two weeks thereafter. Knowing that the holiday season is synonymous with decadence means that you should adjust your offerings to better appease this primed audience, all in the pursuit of greater guest satisfaction and hopefully a few more dollars in your wallet.

As a start, what is mulled wine? Individual recipes vary, but the essential ingredients include red wine, sugar, orange slices, cinnamon and cloves, all stirred together in a simmering pot of deliciousness. The key behind mulled wine's popularity, however, rests not only with its delightful and well-themed flavor but also with its ability to activate other senses in the form of a hot drink (touch) and soothing aromas (smell). Thus, to maximize a consumer's satisfaction with this beverage, your recipe should include the correct proportion of aromatic compounds – to titillate but not overpower the nose – and it should be served in a mug or glass that complements the touch factor.

Alas, though, it wouldn't be the holiday season without a myriad of other sugary alcoholic drinks, first and foremost of which are eggnog and hot buttered rum. Unless you're planning to buy the store-bought premade eggnog, the real thing isn't that hard to whip up from scratch using egg yolks, milk, cream, sugar, vanilla and nutmeg. From there, this love-or-hate-it holiday mixture goes best with rum, Bourbon or Brandy. As its name implies for the latter drink, butter and rum also go great together once you throw in some citrus zest, honey and spices. Our advice for both winter classics is to treat them as the base concoction, then add your own personal touch either in the realm of additive indulgence like whipped cream, caramel swirls and chocolate shavings or unorthodox combinations like eggnog with Fireball Whiskey and a Hot Buttered Rum Affogato.

Next on the savory side are your Irish coffees, alcoholic hot chocolates, White Russians and everything else with Baileys, Crème de Cacao or a coffee liqueur such as Kahlua. Much like our suggestion for eggnog and hot buttered rum, start with a tried-and-true recipe as the foundation before applying your own unique flare to offer diners something that's similar yet different. Three excellent flavor infusions within the given theme are gingerbread, candy cane and peppermint (this last one, lucky for you, already comes in schnapps form).

Moving away from dairy-based brews, think in terms of colors, specifically bright green and scarlet red. The latter is very easy to play with as you can thematically transform a martini, mojito, margarita, mimosa or Moscow Mule (why do all the best cocktails start with the letter M?) into a lucent rouge by introducing a teaspoon of cranberry, raspberry or pomegranate liqueur. Green is a rarer, but not impossible, color to reach, especially when you are working with Crème de Menthe, Chartreuse or anything that's green apple-flavored. And when all else fails, a drop of food coloring can solve any concerns.

Our point throughout all these brief mentions is to get you thinking about what you can do today to give your restaurant that extra bit of vitality for the holidays. When December comes, remember to amplify your spirit selection with a limited assortment of themed drink specials. Make it a fun exercise by getting your team together for a few hours to nail down a few options that aren't a stretch of your existing inventory to create. And any effort you put in now can be revived and expanded upon next year.

Embrace All Fruit

Have you ever tried wine made from blueberries? Or how about sparkling cranberry wine? Wine almost always means grapes, but there are several ways you can use other fruit to boost sales in a restaurant setting through the element of surprise.

Novelty: Some people have more rigid taste buds and will stick with Merlot or Sauvignon Blanc no matter what you say to cajole them. Others might be more daring and try an alchemical tincture of an eclectic fruit if it's on the menu.

Dessert: Again, people come in all shapes and sizes. Some will opt for no dessert; others will order that triple chocolate mousse they've been dreaming of all week long. Others still may forgo cake or pie in favor of a candied libation. Dessert wines are the automatic choice, and then you have Sherry, pear liqueurs and whatever other peculiar concoction that's available.

Mixology: A splash or ounce of wine is a necessary ingredient for many of the more popular cocktails. By using a more obscure fruit wine you are also helping to differentiate your menu and give patrons a flavor they've never quite experienced before.

Jam Tastings: Wines pair exquisitely well with cheeses. The creamy and stinky tasting notes of cheeses also jive with the sugary and tart flavors of various jams. Try matching a Cabernet Sauvignon with a few drops of raspberry jam sprinkled over a chunk of parmesan. Blueberry jam seems to mesh swimmingly with Brie or Camembert. We're sure you can figure out your own suggested pairings, or when you present a cheeseboard to a table just leave a few jams out for people to mix as they see fit. In this way, the food transcends nourishment, becoming a shared interactive experience.

Fruit Pairings: Taking jam one step further, why pair wines and cheeses with a preserve when you could go straight to the source? Using the abovementioned examples, consider pairing a Cabernet Sauvignon with a single, fresh raspberry atop a hunk of firm cheese. Next, go for a crisp Riesling or tart Chardonnay with a lone blueberry embedded into a slice of soft Brie or creamy Camembert.

Experiment: Whether you are dabbling in blueberry wine or finding the best match for a fig jam, the bottom line is that this will require a fair amount of experimentation to discover what works best and what's worth presenting to your patrons. But discovery is part of the fun, and this process is something you shouldn't exclude your customers from either. Perhaps you could leave out a tray of assorted sweet fruits (and potentially some olives for some salty contrast) alongside a cheeseboard to represent a premium appetizer charged per guest, and then let the table decide which combinations they enjoy the most.

Above all, remember that *it's not just food but an experience*. You should aim to give your customers something new, interactive or unexpected. By embracing all fruit, you are opening the doors to many more possibilities that can make the experience even more memorable.

Should You Have Your Own Private Wine Label?

Private labeling of wine at restaurants, clubs or hotel properties can be incredibly lucrative but it also comes with its own set of challenges and caveats. Operators all over the world are already engaged in the practice of *curated wines*, and so to answer the titular question of this chapter: a resounding yes! You should have your own branded wine – one red and one white for a start, and with no premium options – if you understand what you are getting into as it is far from a catch-all solution.

Let's start with the positives. Private labeling gives you complete control from a pricing perspective, allowing you to avoid comparison shopping on the menu because it's a product that's unique to only you. That and your margins will be better.

Second and even more significant are its effects on brand reinforcement. Private labeling means putting your property's name on one more touch point with the consumer, especially one that is connected to a sense beyond mere sight (taste, smell and touch if they pick the bottle up). This brand reinforcement can be further amplified by offering your private label as a gratis, arrival amenity as part of a hotel room package or as a gift to clients or loyal customers. Dovetailing this are the opportunities to expand your brand presence via social media – that is, whenever someone screenshots your label and geotags your restaurant.

The biggest red flag is that private labeling, if done properly, will cannibalize sales of other bottles on the list. As well, there's the potential that such a venture will tarnish your reputation given that the most common perception of private labels is that their quality is equivalent to table wines or low-end stock.

While examples certainly exist at the high end, it will take a lot to change people's minds, especially if you are operating in the haute cuisine or luxury space. We'd recommend that you position your private label not as the lowest retail option but somewhere around the top of bottom quartile of your wine list so that it appeals to neophytes as well as to the more sophisticated drinkers in need of a quick and palatable glass or two.

This is a very broad introduction to the subject of private label, and if you are at least partially convinced reach out to local wineries and vineyards to see if a partnership can be arranged. Such agreements result in supporting the local community where both sides end up winning. And this doesn't have to pertain only to wine, particularly if your business isn't located within or near a growing region. How about private-labeled cheeses? Ditto for breads, snacks, chocolates, confectionaries or whatever else best suites your brand. These branded products are but one more talking point, one more way to enhance the experience.

WINE GROWING
REGIONS

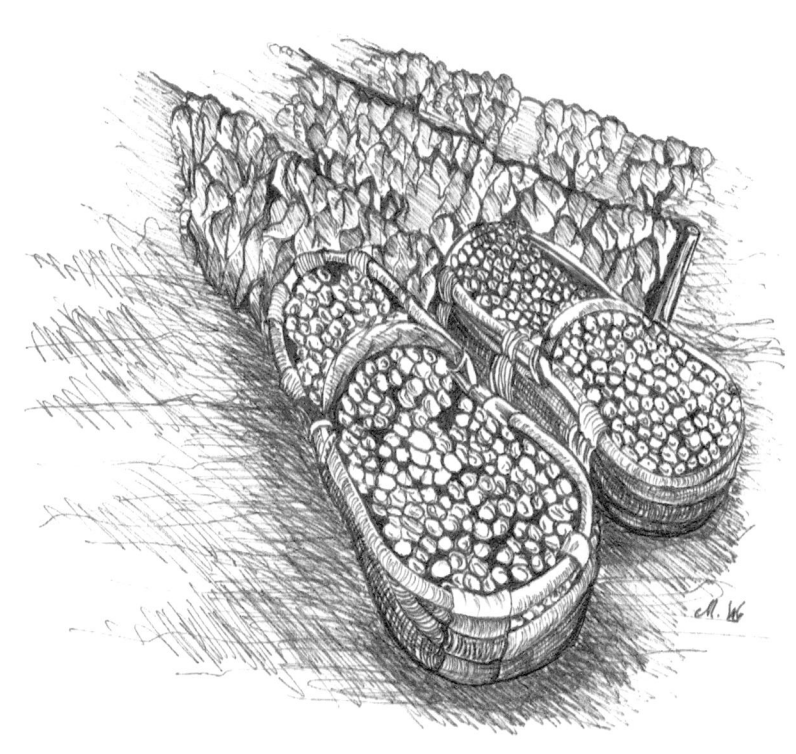

OLD WORLD WINES

Beautiful Bordeaux

Bordeaux in France is perhaps the most prestigious growing region in the world; just don't make that claim to anyone from Burgundy, Italy or NorCal. Bordeaux wines range in price from ten dollars for table drinkers to tens of thousands of dollars for a well-aged *first growth* vintage. Even though these esteemed *premier cru* bottles are mind-blowing in flavor and complexity, Bordeaux has over 7,000+ recognized châteaux, and there are many gems at the mid to low tier. With huge production spread across 60 appellations, it takes a sommelier course to learn all the intricacies of Bordeaux wines. But for the average drinker, most of that doesn't mean anything.

Occupying the southwestern portion of France, Bordeaux is renowned for having the perfect climate for wine – not scorching hot during the summers (well, before climate change) and just the right amount of cool Atlantic breeze. Geographically, what's important to know is that the vineyards are clustered around the banks of two tidal rivers stemming from the Gironde estuary – the Dordogne to the north and the Garonne to the south. Estates north and east of the Dordogne on the 'Right Bank' tend to produce different varietals and blended wines than those on the 'Left Bank' to the south and west of the Garonne (and centered around the actual city of Bordeaux).

Knowing the specific location of the appellation (Left Bank, Right Bank, Between Two Seas/Tides) determines the dominant grape in the blend and will thus play a role in what wine you recommend to a guest. All Bordeaux wines, oaked or not, are a mix of Merlot and Cabernet Sauvignon, with nominal percentages of Cabernet Franc, Malbec and Petit Verdot thrown in for balance and a bit of *je ne sais quoi*. Right Bank wines air towards Merlot dominance, making them softer, fruitier and easier to drink at a younger age. Left Bank bottles are primarily Cabernet Sauvignon, meaning that they are darker and heavier with sharper tannins and better suited for aging.

Bordeaux also produces white varietals, the most notable result being Sauternes dessert wine. Most of these sweet delights are comprised principally of Sémillon with Sauvignon Blanc as a minor constituent and the rare addition of Muscadelle. Outside of Sauternes, when the average person thinks of Bordeaux, his or her first thought is that of excellent tasting reds, so that is where you should focus your attention.

Beyond directing customers to a Cabernet Sauvignon or Merlot-dominant bottle, there are five châteaux to commit to heart – those being the First Growth Bordeaux wines including: Haut-Brion, Lafite Rothschild, Latour, Margaux and Mouton Rothschild. While these may be the most famous, there have been many revisions of the region's classifications to highlight other world-class estates. As such, you might also want to augment your Bordeaux lexicon by knowing a few of the more prominent appellations and communes like Barsac, Graves, Margaux (both a château and a growing commune), Médoc, Pauillac, Pomerol, Saint-Émilion and Sauternes (dual naming for the type of wine as well as the commune).

Once you've gotten used to some of the terminology, you next must ask yourself what it means to have such prestigious wines on your menu. It's unlikely that anyone will ever order a first growth with a price tag of several thousand dollars but stocking them does come with a certain badge of honor. When guests peruse the wine list and see a premier cru at the top of the page, they will think, "Jeez, if this restaurant can shell out for world-class vintages like these then the food must be top notch as well!" It's a form of vicarious status.

That, and the wines taste incredible (or else they wouldn't be worth what they are today). So, while you're pondering whether your restaurant needs a boost of Bordeaux's 'prestige by proxy', try a bottle yourself, if only to test the purple waters so to speak. And as a resolution, be sure to educate your servers on the region's wine story because if they can get patrons excited about Bordeaux, then it'll translate to a healthy flow of beverage revenues.

Bold Ol' Burgundy

Behind Bordeaux, one of the foremost appellation regions in France is Burgundy. Lying roughly in the middle latitudes of the eastern half of the nation and catching the tail end of the Rhône River in the northwestern Alps, Burgundy makes some of the best and most acclaimed wines in the world, with a proud viticulture dating back to the first Roman settlements of the area.

Before all of us started spending real money on bottles, our introductory wine classifications were likely generalized by country name – France, Italy, Austria and so on. But once we graduated to the next level or assumed roles as servers, somms or hoteliers, we became keenly aware of the serious differences in winemaking and taste from appellation to appellation, beginning with the grape varietals that are grown. Burgundy terroir and wines are heavily controlled, and, with only a few exceptions, their reds are made from Pinot Noir and whites from Chardonnay.

To us, Burgundy defines Old World flavor. The reds are dry, savory and multilayered. The whites are spritely, tangy and rich with none of the domineering sugariness or fruitiness of New World crushes. In fact, both Pinot Noir and Chardonnay were bred and matured into their distinct contemporary lineages in this region.

Our love of Burgundy peaked when we toured the Côte-d'Or Department (as subregions are called in France) in style via hot air balloon, floating from vineyard to vineyard and sampling the world's finest drops alongside some mouthwatering cheeses and snacks. On a tangent, worth tasting are Burgundy's many Dijon mustards and its rustic stew, beef bourguignon, as well as its Époisses cheese, an off-orange-colored, stinky, salty and soft cheese with a pink-dusted washed rind dubbed the 'king of cheese' by Napoleon. It truly lives up to this name. This trip was far from inexpensive we might add.

The Côte-d'Or happens to be the epicenter for reputable winemaking in the region, all codified under the *grand cru* system as the stamp of supreme quality pertaining exclusively to Burgundy wines. If you're fortunate enough to get your hands on a grand cru (only about 1-2% of total bottles from the Burgundy region) savor every drop as this mark of distinction is not handed out lightly; you are drinking one of best wines in the whole wide world. Secondary wines are classified as premier cru, followed by the specific region in Burgundy as an Appellation d'Origine Contrôlée (AOC).

The best of the best of Burgundy is known as DRC or Domaine de la Romanée-Conti. These wines are not just some of the finest in the world but are so sought after that they hold records at auction houses that quite literally make them worth more by weight than pure gold.

With this as a lead in, if you want your wine menu to connote the same esteem and sophistication as your cuisine, segregating your French listings by regional subsections is a must. Think Burgundy, Bordeaux, Côte du Rhône and Loire Valley at the big four – wholly permissible because of the tight controls on grape varietal production within each region and the distinctive flavors that result.

Stocking one or two grand cru bottles, although quite expensive, is an important investment for celebratory cases where a group is commemorating a very special moment in someone's life. And indeed, if you want to attract special occasion customers, you need wines worthy of the moment. With only a dozen or so grand cru bottles in our cellar, we can remember every time they have been consumed. The last one? Larry's 65th birthday included a 2000 Ruchottes-Chambertin.

Look to the Loire

As a wine producer, France is so much more than Bordeaux and Burgundy – its two most prestigious growing regions and perhaps the only two that most people can name offhand. Wherever you can harvest grapes, the French are already doing just that, and there are many fantastic hidden gems (sometimes at bargain prices) waiting for you and your guests to discover, thereby helping increase meal satisfaction and revenue per table.

From a North American perspective, the Loire Valley isn't as well-known. While your patrons yearn for a bit of education to enrich their dining experiences, they don't want to be force-fed a lecture. As such, when introducing an appellation, varietal, winemaking process or anything else from the vintner's glossary of terms, start simple then expand only when prompted. What we've previously alluded to as a wine or growing region's USP; the one for the Loire would sound something along the lines of, "A growing region in Northwestern France that happens to be the birthplace of Sauvignon Blanc."

While the appellations around the Loire River are also the place of origin for Cabernet Franc, Chenin Blanc and Muscadet, everyone has at least a vague concept of Sauvignon Blanc, so the above sentence is readily accepted. As a northern region about two-thirds the size of Bordeaux and covering a vast swath of geography from the Atlantic through to the heart of the country, the summers are shorter and the climate is far from

Mediterranean in composition, meaning that the taste profiles for the product are substantially different.

Whereas the wines from Languedoc-Roussillon, Provence or even into Spain and Italy are renowned for their thick and pungent Old World flavors, Loire bottles tend to have a more muted, low sugar and low acid palate – a direct reflection of the climate and terroir. Nowhere is this more apparent than the citrusy yet highly subdued Sauvignon Blancs from the better-known appellations of Pouilly Fumé and Sancerre. But this light-bodied quality extends to the Pinot Noir, Rosé and Cabernet Franc made further down the river.

Unlike, for instance, Burgundy where the region is dominated by one grape for red and one for white, the Loire Valley has a diverse range of single varietals in use. To get people interested and to sell a few more glasses in the process, though, look to what is exceptional.

The Sauvignon Blanc from the Upper Loire are bar none the best in the world, so if you put one or two on the list, the argument for their purchase is easy – the best expression of this grape. Likewise, Cabernet Franc from this part of the globe, especially from the centrally situated Chinon AOC, are irreplaceable while Muscadet and Melon de Bourgogne varietals are as unique as they come.

The same cannot be said, however, for sparkling whites from Saumur or Vouvray, which, although made from the rarer Chinon Blanc grape, must compete for name recognition with the likes of Champagne and Prosecco. Thus, unless your restaurant is called 'Bubbles' and specializes in the full range of these crude, dry, semisweet and sweet doubly fermented elixirs, stick to the brands with more ingrained awareness and leave the Loire to its most special of specialties.

Tuscan Titans

Now that we've touched upon our favorite wine regions in France, it's time to move on to Italy, and specifically Tuscany, probably the country's foremost producer. Located north of Rome proper along the Tyrrhenian Sea, this region of Italy (which we've visited on a couple occasions) is marked by its idyllic rolling hills of verdant green fields abutting centuries-old, fortified towns of well-preserved brickwork, clay and timeless artistry.

This land is the home to three very popular tourist cities – Florence, Pisa and Siena – although nearly every other town or *agriturismo* offers yet one more reason to fall in love with the land.

It goes without saying that Tuscany (and all the nations surrounding the Mediterranean) has a longstanding viticultural footprint, dating back to before the Roman conquest of the Italian Peninsula. During the Dark Ages, it was the pious monks who took the reins amidst the economic collapse of Western Europe. The current iterations by which we classify this nation's pedigrees today emerged during the early Renaissance when Northern Italian city-states awoke as European centers of commerce, bringing with them lots of fresh capital and a renewed demand for expensive wine.

Nowadays, much like in France, Italy adheres to a scrupulous set of quality assurance protocols for its growing regions. Look for the DOC or, even better, the DOCG label to ensure that you're getting a traditional Tuscan product. The emphasis here is that of quality over quantity, which means that, when combined with the semi-arid climate and the thin layer of topsoil, Tuscany has a very low yield relative to other Italian regions. Not surprisingly, four-fifths of what's made are red varietals.

Our experiences with Tuscan wines pertain mostly to that of Brunello, Chianti and Vino Nobile di Montepulciano (not to be confused with the Montepulciano made in Abruzzo). All three of these wines are made almost entirely from the Sangiovese grape, bestowing them with an opaque red-violet color and a fruity, full-bodied taste. This consistency in flavor means that Tuscan reds are great for pairings – a rich, tannin-heavy, acidic drop matches perfect with any pizza, tomato-based pasta, red meat like Bistecca Fiorentina or savory, spicy dishes like Peposo.

Aside from our own personal preferences and all the other varietals beyond the scope of this cursory coverage, we have only two quick suggestions. First, for novices, the Italian grape, vineyard and appellation names can be quite intimidating, especially because of the language barrier. Look for ways to simplify or explain your Tuscan wine selection on the menu to reduce confusion and help with a sale. Better yet, lend a bit of knowledge to your servers so that they can extend their interactions with your patrons and heighten the rapport.

Second, Tuscan wines are amongst the most popular and sought after in the world. Ergo, getting your hands on quality product is easier said than done or, at the very least, will require a healthy upfront investment. Once you throw in the appropriate markups, you will be asking your customers for quite a lot of dough for each bottle, a number which might frighten more than a few people who have no clue what they're getting.

As such, consider how Tuscans fit into the bigger picture of your wine list. Do they connote the top end of your selection, reserved for a select few? Or, if your restaurant caters to a more casual crowd, perhaps you could source from some of the more inexpensive Chianti labels. If you're lucky, you can even connect with a budding producer of 'Super Tuscan' wines which breach the DOC rules because they blend international grapes like Cabernet Sauvignon and Merlot in with the Sangiovese for some truly enchanting results.

Piedmont Power

For those of you who haven't visited Italy yet, fake an illness and hop on the next flight. Well, maybe don't go that far, but as Italophiles we staunchly support you putting the country on your bucket list. The beauty of Italy lies with its vast depth of history and culture as well as the exceptional qualities of its individual regions. Remember that Italy as a modern, unified nation has only existed for just over 150 years.

One of these regions is the Piedmont in the northwest, centered on the city of Turin with the main growing regions in Monferrato around the cities of Asti and Alessandria. For a very long time, it was a part of the Duchy of Savoy, meaning that it still has many cultural links to France. As far as winemaking goes, the previous chapter on Tuscany covered what is first to mind for North Americans, but the Piedmont is more than its equal with Barolo, Barbaresco, Dolcetto, Langhe Nebbiolo and many other excellent varietals made here.

To understand the Piedmont is to first know that the region has some of the best geography for viticulture. Its flat grasslands and rolling hills are ringed by the Alps in the north and west, and the Ligurian range in the south (separating it from the Genovese coast). All told, these mountains effectively trap the summer heat with sunny, humid days easily passing

40C – conditions that also happens to be perfect for concentrating sugars and flavor within the region's thick-skinned grapes.

What's important to keep in mind with these varietals is that the wines take a long time to mature, and the taste shows substantial changes year-over-year. The cream of the crop, in our opinion is a decent Barolo, with its hearty, tar-filled drop that can take a decade to reach the semblance of maturity – best paired with meats and other heavy cream-laden dishes. The Dolcetto exudes a tangy, fruity red flavor, perfect for pomodoro pizzas, light pastas, spicy foods or strong parmesan-esque cheeses. Hungry yet?

The Piedmont has many other excellent budget-oriented bottles worth a taste or a purchase. Many of the reds are based on the Nebbiolo (which translates as 'fog'), Barbera and the Moscato Bianco which is the basis for the ultra-sweet Champagne usurper Moscato D'Asti.

We could go on and on about the wonders of Piedmont wine, but the only way to get to know this region is to experience it yourself, ideally by traveling there or, as a runner up, visiting your local liquor store and sampling a few bottles.

Like many other countries with a strong viticultural heritage, Italy also has many proud culinary traditions with each region contributing their own delicacies and unique dishes to the overall picture. In North America, Italian cuisine is often lumped into the broad, countrywide categories of antipasti, insalate, pizze, paste, primi, secondi and dolci. Even using the traditional Italian pluralization for each word doesn't excite the eyes, chiefly because every other bistro, osteria, pizzeria, trattoria and ristorante is doing the same thing.

Instead, how about arranging the menu items according to their respective region of origin? Then, of course, wine, as a fantastic complement to any such dinner, would also be matched accordingly. This makes sense because the cuisine of each region in Italy evolved symbiotically with its traditional wines, making pairings second nature.

So, you could have a Barolo or Moscato paired on the page with Piedmont specialties like Bagna Cauda or, as a dessert, some Gianduja (chocolate and hazelnut). Or how about a Ligurian white matched with some of Genoa's other homegrown creations like Focaccia with pesto or Salsa di Noci (walnut sauce)? Similarly, Milanese cuisine is renowned for its risottos and ossobuco. The opportunities for crafting a hyper-regional culinary experience abound.

Hardly is this concept exclusive to Italy. Why can't you do the same with, say, a French café? In this case, you might bifurcate the menu into Provençal and Lyonnaise haute cuisine, and Northern French and Breton dishes. Yes, there is the possibility of confusion, but the greater idea here is to be different with a specific, well-guided story, and therein create an impression.

Victory in Veneto

What do you have on your bucket list? You know you're a true wine lover when one on yours is an annual convention called *Vinitaly* held every April in the city of Verona in the heart of the region of Veneto. Behind Tuscany and Piedmont is the ostensible 'third place' for Italian growing regions – that of Veneto which covers a wide swath of land from the Adriatic Coast around Venice in the northeast to the foothills of Alps.

While some will likely take umbrage with our tertiary ranking of this region – as everyone has their own personal favorites – know that it is based on each territory's current prestige and, to a lesser extent, the bottle prices of top local wineries. While Piedmont and Tuscany are in a perpetual battle to be the most expensive that Italy has to offer, what firmly puts Veneto in third and ahead of the other 17 regions in Italy is Amarone.

Made from partially dried grapes left out for months on straw mats, a bit of noble rot is allowed to accumulate and lend its glycerol flavor to the final product. A bottle of 'big bitter' (as the direct translation of Amarone) offers customers a distinctively crisp flavor that also has a high alcohol content. A worthy upper-snack-bracket addition to any wine list, Amarone has a great taste that pairs well with everything from pastas and fish to chicken, pork or practically any other protein. Moreover, the *appassimento* or partial drying process gives this wine a good story for your servers to convey to enrich the meal experience.

Beyond this Venetian hallmark, lest we forget that although Veneto is third overall in total vineyard area, it is first in total production. The area's more quotidian fare from Valpolicella is on par with Chianti and Nebbiolo, both in terms of production scale as well as quality. Literally meaning 'valley of many cellars', the quintessential namesake red blend is light, dry and easy drinking.

Then there is the only recently popular *ripasso* style which involves adding the pomace from other production lines – for instance, the leftover solid waste from making Amarone – back into the fermentation pot with the rest of the slowly macerating grapes to bestow the resultant wine with more tannins and complexity.

If you are looking for a white to accompany these noteworthy reds, Veneto has plenty to offer with almost two-thirds of the region devoted to white wine production. Soave should be first on your list, though, with a semi-aromatic flavor profile designed to complement any locally produced cheeses (Asiago and Grana Padano both made nearby) or charcuterie. Lastly, Prosecco also hails from Veneto is you are looking to round out your menu with a sparkler, particularly now that this wine is a common ingredient in numerous boozy brunch accompaniments.

While Veneto surely has a lot to offer, the overarching lesson is that you must start to think about infusing more specific geographic references and themes to your operations. It was more than enough two decades ago to be the proprietor of an Italian restaurant, but nowadays that blanket national identifier isn't enough to differentiate your product. Instead, you might describe one of your food outlets as Roman, Tuscan, Piedmontese, Milanese or Venetian. The more specific you get with your theme and culinary offerings, the greater the narrative, memorability and overall meal satisfaction.

A Campaign for Spain

In North America, Spanish wines and grapes are often not as popular as their French or Italian counterparts while the country's native varietals aren't as well-known as the international flights of Cabernet Sauvignon, Chardonnay, Malbec, Merlot, Pinot Noir, Sauvignon Blanc and Syrah.

This sentiment is quite understandable when you consider that until the mid 1970s, Spain under the Franco regime didn't have a federal body in charge of viticultural modernization, nor the capitalist fervor needed for competitive winemaking. Prior to the country's emergence as a free market economy, most of the alcoholic produce was locally consumed and, frankly, jug wine at best. Nowadays, however, Spain is still a top consumer, but it's also the third largest exporter, and some of its labels are arguably able to contend with the best of the world.

When it comes to introducing the specifics and peculiarities of Spanish wine, largely because of its relative isolation from the rest of the world through the post-World War II trading boom, there are now dozens of unfamiliar grape and growing region names, not to mention the Iberian Peninsula's wildly diverse geography. As we know by now, too much too soon results in blank stares and an information retention rate close to zero. The campaign for Spain requires a slow introduction. For now, we'll discuss only the wines that most distinctively embody the nation's output and, more importantly, the ones most likely to sell.

Looking at Spain from a satellite, its features are quite remarkable. The Iberian Peninsula is sliced by a series of mountain ranges, creating substantial rain shadows around the river valley systems where grapevines like to prosper. These cordilleras as they are called protect Spain's interior plateau, the Meseta Central, bestowing the lands with a continental Mediterranean climate (think extreme heat with sporadic droughts in summer) as well as those quixotic images of endless golden fields with brown and ochre mountaintops in the background. Indeed, these rich, volcanic soils have been recognized for viticultural purposes even before the Roman conquests, first undertaken by Phoenician and Carthaginian colonists.

Winegrowing dots the entirety of the Spanish countryside, save for the most arid regions of the Meseta Central. In the spotlight are two within the watershed of the Ebro River – Rioja and Priorat – near or in the Catalan province that stretches from the Iberian coast up to the Pyrenees. Like other Mediterranean-facing countries, Spain has a regulatory body for good wines (Denominación de Origen – DO), but both Priorat and Rioja are of such renown that they have earned a superior classification (DOQ) while a 'DO de Pago' sticker is reserved for internationally celebrated estates or wineries ('bodegas' as they are locally called).

La Rioja sits more inland, immediately south of the Cantabrian Mountains that separate it from Basque Country and some rather fierce Northern Atlantic storms. The vineyards atop this limestone and sandstone plateau are best known for growing *tintos* (red grapes), especially

Tempranillo. To the layman, this varietal can be described as a thicker, coarser Merlot, delivering a burst of leather and sandalwood from its intense, dark crimson color. Tempranillo is popular throughout the north of Spain, and it is usually the dominant grape in a blend with Garnacha (Grenache) or Monastrell (Mourvèdre).

If most regions are making Tempranillo, what makes Rioja so special? What makes their wines worth the higher price? The region has its own internal categorization system, and you should strive for Rioja Reserva or Rioja Gran Reserva markers because they denote a minimum number of years aging in American or French oak barrels, specifically adding a smoky vanilla.

At this point we must admit that we're biased towards Spanish reds, and even though Spain has some delectable whites (Airén, Albariño, Macabeo or Verdejo), our experience has mostly been with their darker counterparts. In the Priorat region, which lies directly southwest of the Catalonian coastline, the big red on campus is Garnacha Tinta where, again, blending is the order of the day. Elsewhere in the world (mainly the Rhône River valley), Grenache is usually the runner-up in a blend, but in Spain it takes centerstage, delivering a heavy body of sweet, black fruit and spicy tannins.

To finish off, what would a rambling about Spanish wine be without mentioning Sangria? Like most traditional dishes or drinks that we now extol, Sangria is comprised of whatever was typically left lying around in a Spanish kitchen. A summer delight, a pitcher is an easy medley of red wine (or sometimes white if that's all you have left), a bit of syrup or sugar, some Brandy or Sherry, chopped fruit, carbonated soda and ice. If you offer Spanish reds by the glass, you might as well add Sangria to the menu, especially during the warmer months. It's fun and a pitcher can add a communal aspect to the dining experience much like a charcuterie board.

Port and Portuguese Wines

While discussing Spain, it would seem only fair that we freshen up on our knowledge of the other nation within the Iberian Peninsula. While the coastal nation of Portugal currently holds the 11th spot in global production – falling a couple hundred thousand tonnes short of Germany which has drastically ramped up production in the past decade – its influence is less so marked by exceptional vintages with prices through the stratosphere like those from Bordeaux, California or the Piedmont and more so by its superb, fortified wines.

Named after the city of Porto (which also gives the country its namesake) where all barrels were stored prior to dissemination upon the high seas, port wines run the gamut of dry, semi-sweet, sweet, ruby, white, tawny, vintage or late-bottled vintage. Even though port has fallen out of favor in recent years as an aperitif or digestif, its comeback is all but unavoidable.

But before we validate this claim, some history, geography and terroir are in order. Despite what may have come off as a bit of a snub in the opening paragraph, Portugal does indeed boast some great reds and whites, just that they haven't yet reached the same renown as other nations. Vines are cultured throughout the country, but the most prized area is also the oldest.

While wine has been a part of the economy since Roman times, modern viticulture only really took off once the Douro Valley (Duero in Spanish) in the northeast was recognized for its superior goods around the same time as Chianti in Tuscany and Tokaji in Hungary some three-and-a-half centuries ago. This region is sheltered from the untamed Atlantic weather patterns by high mountains and steep valleys, with terraced vineyards built upon the antediluvian granite-rich soil to make it well-suited for most Mediterranean varietals. However, due to the country's relative isolation from the rest of Europe, it developed its most common varietals internally, all with Portuguese names that we need not confuse you with for this cursory overview.

Where we leave you here on this matter is for you to experiment with a couple whites or reds offered on the menu, knowing that there are absolutely some great drops for reasonable prices coming from the Douro Valley or other growing regions like the Dão River or the Minho province in the far northwest with its perfectly crushable Vinho Verde.

Port wine is what put the nation on the map, however, and this is where we can see your restaurant seizing the moment with healthy returns. The fortified liquor is made via a process called *mutage* whereby a high percentage spirit is added partway through fermentation, which kills off the yeast and halts any further chemical digestion. This leaves lots of residual sugars and an alcohol proportion hovering around 20%. It's this combination of sweetness and lower ABV compared to other grape-based spirits like Brandy, Cognac or Grappa that make port an ideal alternative for lunch, casual afternoon affairs, aperitifs, cocktail mixtures and dessert accompaniments where the objective is to not get completely sloshed.

Of course, different occasions call for different Ports. Tawny Ports, which are those made from red grapes and left in wooden barrels long enough for thorough oxidation of the originally claret color, usually pair best with nutty flavors like strong cheeses or desserts on the more 'savory' end of the spectrum like dark chocolate, eggy pastries, custards or pecan pie. Vintages for Ports are unusual in that not every year is denoted as such, and the 'best of best' bottles should be reserved for solo enjoyment either before or after the meal. A final word to the wise for bartenders is that Ports are unlike other hard liquors; once you pop, the fun does eventually stop. Port oxidizes like regular wine, albeit slower, so use it and charge for it accordingly.

While high-end Ports stand on their own as versatile beverages, we will soon witness the rise in popularity of white or ruby port cocktails which harness the wine's sweetness to balance out stronger additives and bitters. As the cheapest of its kind, the ruby bottles are best for mixing, with everything from port-colored cocktails and lemonade blends for those hot summer days to Mimosa-like blends with sparkling white wines and Sangria made with port instead of the typical red plonk. We were first nudged towards port's concoctive ability during a business trip to San Francisco when we stopped by the Sir Francis Drake Hotel and sampled one of their patented 'Drake Manhattans' which expertly infuses a tawny port with the customary mainstays of whiskey (Bourbon in this case) and a dash of bitters along with a spoonful of maple syrup.

The question from all this is how are you going to leverage port to enhance your beverage menu? Furthermore, how are you going to inspire your in-house mixologists to infuse fortified wine into their cocktails? And if you think along the lines of 'Drake Manhattan', what drink will your hotel become known for? To this last one, port may just be the ticket to reaching similar levels of distinction.

As a final aside, no discussion of Port and Portuguese wine would be complete without the mention of Madeira, the tropical Atlantic outcrop halfway between the Azores and the Canary Islands that produces an eponymous fortified wine that is rusty bronze to amber in color, also around 20% alcohol and another great addition to your dessert list or as a cocktail additive. Lesser-known menu supplements like Madeira are not only uniquely flavorful but are also great conversation starters for an even more memorable dining occasion.

German Giants

For those of you who can't take the time off work to travel to Munich for Oktoberfest, there's a lot you can do to bring the spectacle home for your guests to enjoy, both for the duration of this quintessential German celebration and for the rest of the year.

The title of this book denotes wine, but our first thoughts about Germany and Oktoberfest obviously lean far closer towards beer. After all, the nation does have a proud and deep-rooted heritage of brewing, so you will never be buying bland beer by stocking one or more golden lagers from the big six sponsor breweries (Augustiner-Bräu, Hacker-Pschorr, Hofbräu, Löwenbräu, Paulaner and Spaten-Franziskaner-Bräu).

Outside of Bavaria exists a plethora of delicious beers of all varieties including white (Weiss), wheat (Weizen), Pilsner, Lager, dark ales (Dunkel) and stouts (Schwarz). These are perfect for any themed Oktoberfest party you might plan for your restaurant or as a regular addition to the menu. Keep in mind that many Old World breweries don't add preservatives or other artificial ingredients (in Germany, abiding by the Reinheitsgebot) and as such their serviceable delivery range is quite limited. But this detriment comes with the lofty benefit of enhanced flavor.

German wines shouldn't be sidelined either. Many of their varietals and vineyards rival those of the more preeminent wine-producing European nations of France or Italy, even though the volume isn't quite there. The fact remains that, like the rest of the Mediterranean, Germany has been making wine since Roman times. In the modern era, they've been especially proactive in bringing their quality up to par with that of the leading winemakers.

Most German wines are produced along the Rhine and its tributaries in the western states, with breathtaking landscapes of vineyards on steep 45-to-70-degree verdant hills abutting the broad waterways. If you ever have the opportunity, take a cruise along the Middle Rhine starting approximately at Koblenz where vineyards and lush forests mix with preserved medieval towns, cathedrals and hilltop castles.

To keep things simple, the dominant grapes to remember are Riesling, Pinot Gris (locally known as Grauburgunder), Silvaner and Müller-Thurgau for the whites, and Pinot Noir (called Spätburgunder) and Dornfelder for the reds.

As both Pinots are more appropriately discussed in relation to French and Burgundian wines, the centerpiece of any German selection should be a Riesling (the second most-produced white, Müller-Thurgau, is based off the Riesling and shares many of its properties). Typically sweet, dry, acerbic and with a pungent dose of citrus fruits, these wines pair best with seafood, pork, cream-based sauces or spicy dishes. A tad more unusual, Silvaner can be compared to the main Austrian varietal, Grüner Veltliner, with a milder, floral taste great for chicken, fowl or desserts.

And when it comes to Oktoberfest and delivering a genuine German experience, you might also want to consider throwing in a few local dishes as accompaniments. Think sauerkraut (fermented cabbage) and bratwurst (grilled sausages), but also knödel (potato dumplings), sauerbraten (pot roast), rotkohl (braised red cabbage) or pretzels with horseradish mustard as a snack. German cuisine is very filling and when paired with a hearty lager or glass of wine, you can't go wrong.

Austrian Edelweiss

When it comes to Austrian viticulture, we are more-or-less talking the lowland regions in and around Vienna in the eastern half of the country bordering Slovakia and Hungary – the Weinland Österreich. Even though this nation might not have the same lofty prestige as Mediterranean-facing vintners, the winemaking heritage nonetheless predates Roman times.

And it shows! With strict laws in place and a shrewd focus on quality over quantity, there's no reason why Austrian wines shouldn't grace your menu. This pursuit of grape excellence also means that Austria is only the 16th largest producer by volume in the world (where France and Italy are first and second respectively), which plays a hand in both elevating the prices for bottles and their rarity. Due to this second point, simply having an Austrian label on the wine list may be enough to pique the interest of a more adventurous patron.

The prototypical contemporary Austrian varietal is that of a dry yet full-bodied white with Grüner Veltliner leading the pack at just over a third of all grapes grown in the country. Living up to its namesake ('grüner' means 'green', and this single word often serves as the namesake), wines of this pedigree have a crisp, acidic tang with strong notes of lime zest, nectarine, tart apple and pepper.

The Grüner has gained a lot of traction amongst oenophiles in recent years because its well-balanced mixture of dry flavors means that it can pair with savory as well as highly bitter foods. Think chicken schnitzel with a side of rapini; normally you would put a red in this picture, but a Grüner will work just fine. Along these lines, this varietal can also be paired with any hearty meat or shellfish as well as sharp spices like ginger, tarragon, dill or curry.

As for other whites, be on the lookout for Welschriesling which, although unrelated to the more prevalent German or Rhine Riesling, can produce some equally sweet and fruity wines while also having a tawny coloration in sharp contrast to the pale greens of the Grüner. The Müller-Thurgau or Rivaner – a hybrid strain very popular in German vineyards – has made substantial inroads in Austria, producing a light, semisweet taste much like Sauvignon Blanc (and it is paired similarly, too).

When it comes to reds, which are far less widespread than whites, Zweigelt is the most common grape used, known for its bright violet-red color and soft tannins with a taste likened to a spicy, aromatic Pinot Noir – perfect for peppery meats, strong cheeses and anything tomato-based. Next worth mention is the Blauburger. Its dark, deep purple color is contrasted by its velvety and rather neutral berry taste profile. Blauburger is often matched with roasted vegetables, pork dishes or anything based in a mustard or creamy mushroom sauce.

Lastly, Austria is known for its incredibly syrupy dessert wines mostly coming from the area around Lake Neusiedl, but as is the case with nearly every Austrian varietal grown, local consumption (amounting to roughly three-quarters of what's produced) prevents the export market from truly blossoming for anything outside of the Grüner Veltliner. As such, start with this 'green' white, working it into the wine list and pairings, and then, only if the demand is there, explore further.

I Heard It Through the Greece Vine

If a nation happens to have an ancient god of wine, then you know that grapes are indeed important to the culture. Such is the case with Greece, one of the oldest wine-producing regions in the world and home to our dearest, drunkest Dionysus. In fact, it was in Hellenic heartland where our modern breed of grapevine was developed and perfected for growth in the dry summers, ample sunlight and mild winters of the Mediterranean.

While the country pales in comparison to the three big of Europe (Italy, France and Spain) in terms of total output, that hardly precludes it from offering many eloquent drops. Greece currently boasts more than 300 varietals from 28 designated growing regions, all with quite uncommon names. This means that whatever your choice of acquisition from this land, the label is destined to be a niche product and a head-scratcher for almost all patrons who come across it on a wine list. Some will be more adventurous and seek out esoteric bottles from smaller countries like Greece while others will be outright intimidated and stick to the more internationally renowned grapes.

Greek wines make a good case for appealing to people's sense of heritage. After all, who wouldn't want to share a bottle from a region with over 6,000 years of winemaking? For terroir, many Greek wines are cultivated on islands laden with volcanic ash-rich soil, imparting a distinctive earthy flavor and minerality that's unmatched anywhere else in the world. Further, many of these same islands were unperturbed by the phylloxera blight of the latter half of the 19th century, meaning that several of the nation's varietals in use today are truly original in terms of delivering a quintessentially firm and acidic Old World taste. That's a selling point.

As for the four grapes to remember, these are Assyrtiko, Moschofilero, Agiorgitiko and Xinomavro, two whites and two reds respectively. Originally from the former volcano that is now the island Santorini, Assyrtiko is a steely, aromatic (and phylloxera-resistant) white with dry, citrus-blossom characteristics like Riesling. Second comes Moschofilero which is lighter and quite floral relative to Assyrtiko, making it a better match for desserts or sugar-dominant snacking foods.

On the darker side, Agiorgitiko is the most popular export, with a transparent ruby body and composite flavor profile akin to Pinot Noir. Xinomavro, the other red, is bolder with its opaque violet color and generous burst of sour fruit and tannins in the same vein as many reds from Piedmont. It also ages quite well if you're looking to sit on some cases for a few years.

We could go into more detail here, but this is the basics that your servers should be able to quickly pass on to guests. Any information beyond this can be quite intimidating and should be left for the aficionados and sommeliers amongst us. And if you haven't tried a Greek wine yet, do Dionysus proud and pour yourself a glass!

Eastern European Wines

When your picture a vineyard in your minds, your first thoughts are probably going to be along the lines of bucolic, sunbaked hills beset against a lush Californian or Mediterranean backdrop. And yet, ingenuity is happening in small pockets across the globe that is allowing for some rather tasty bottles to emerge.

While some people may consider Austria and Greece as a part of Central or Eastern Europe, we've already covered those two nations in previous chapters. This entry concerns Hungry, Romania, Bulgaria and, to a certain extent, the Balkans, all with quintessentially continental climates. That's quite a bit of territory to cover, but as your guests are concerned, you only need a superficial level of knowledge, largely because many of the names are unusual and thus intimidating to the average Western consumer.

Up until a few years ago, if you were to ask us about wines from this region, we'd be drawing a big white blank. But where there's lack, there's also the opportunity for learning, especially given the fact that Eastern European wines are still yet to peak.

What convinced us of the potential for finding some truly exquisite drops within these developing nations was a sturdy reminder that the entirety of this region below the Danube was once Roman land and the imperialists were quick to import their viticultural traditions. Romanian is, after all, a Romance language with many of its words derived from Latin.

Not only do Eastern European wines still boast many of the same growing practices and vine lineages as their ancient Greek and Italian trading partners, but, ever since of the collapse of the Soviet bloc, capitalistic enterprises have also flourished, resulting in vastly increased production and better tasting products overall. Let's brush over a few highlights so that you in turn can better sell these exotic and relatively inexpensive bottles.

Starting with the 13th largest producing country, Romania, its three named wine regions are Murfatlar adjacent to the Black Sea, and Dealu Mare and Târnave on the southern slopes of the Carpathian Mountains, all of which have widespread penetration of the international grapes. In this sense, you might consider stocking a familiar varietal from a strange land to ease guests into the purchase. But higher quality indigenous varietals like Fetească Neagră, Fetească Albă, Negru de Drăgăşani and Tămâioasă Românească are emerging as niche exports (easy names to remember as 'neagra' and 'alba' denote black and white respectively while the third has the country's namesake in it).

The best way to sell Romanian wine is to appeal to a patron's sense of heritage; they have been perfecting their craft for thousands of years. The region has now almost fully recovered from the cultivation hiccup that was the latter half of the 20th century, but the prices have yet to keep pace relative to quality. This vending notion also extends to the wines of most other European Eastern nations like Moldova, Georgia and Armenia, where jug wine producers are slowly upgrading their practices for a better-tiered selection.

Next on the highlight reel is Hungary, and for all intents and purposes this comes to whites, sparkling wines and dessert wines from the renowned Tokaj region which is a volcanic-soiled plateau in the northeast with a well-shielded microclimate resulting from its location within the concavity of the crescent-shaped Carpathian Mountains. The only other prestigious contributor worth mentioning at a glance is the Bull's Blood of Eger – Egri Bikavér in the local tongue – as a bold red blend of Germanic and French varietals.

Although dry Tokaji are beginning to make an impression on the marketplace, when these Hungarian wines are mentioned, it is assumed that the discussion will pertain to the nectar-sweet bottles made from Furmint, Muscat and Hárslevelü grapes, often harvested around November and nobly rotted for enhanced sugar concentration. Many Tokaji have a topaz or stark amber coloration which can be used as an additional selling point as they offer a visual demarcation from other whites and thus the heightened perception of a distinguished drinking experience.

Tokaj wines' stellar reputation isn't built on mere hype; they taste fantastic! Of all the nomenclature thrown around in this section, if you had to choose just one cellar addition, you would most likely opt for a Tokaji. They're consistent and they have the most recognizable name. A caveat before you stock up: these wines are incredibly sweet. In fact, much like French Champagnes, they are graded on a sweetness scale. Be sure to test out your comfort zone (as well as that of your customers) on this scale before purchasing in bulk.

Moving deeper into the Balkan Peninsula, we arrive at Bulgaria. Even though their reputation as a producer has slid in the past few decades, lest we forget that their winemaking traditions were incubated by Greek colonists many centuries before the Romans arrived. Much like the effects of the Carpathians, the Balkan Mountain Range, which horizontally bifurcates the nation, also acts as a barrier from the cold continental winds sweeping off the Eurasian Steppe. Aside from a heavy penetration of international varietals, the foremost hero worth stocking comes via the Mavrud grape. Originating from the Greek word for black (which also lends itself to the popular Greek wine, Xinomavro), Mavrud bottles are both highly tannic and quite spicy.

Without overstaying our welcome, we hope this is enough to entice you to consider perusing Eastern European wines for your guests when your cellar starts running low. There are quite a few hidden gems for bargain prices, and the quality will only continue to improve as modern practices take root.

NEW WORLD WINES

Returning to NorCal

NorCal, short for Northern California, produces ostensibly the best wines in North America. Ever since Chateau Montelena's Chardonnay beat out the longstanding French incumbents in a blind taste test in Paris in 1976 (the 2008 film *Bottle Shock* portrays these events if you're in need of a lighthearted wine-themed movie), Napa Valley and Californian wines have been on an upward spiral of fame, flavor and price. Nowadays, the very mention of the word 'Napa' is synonymous with quality.

Geopolitically, NorCal is traditionally defined as stretching from Monterrey County just south of the Bay Area north to the Oregon border. When it comes to wine, we are primarily talking Napa and Sonoma Valleys, and to a lesser extend Mendocino and Lake County, all officially encompassed under the North Coast American Viticultural Area (AVA). This distinguishes it from the Central Coast AVA which encompasses all vineyards south of San Francisco through to Santa Barbara.

Our purpose with writing about NorCal is not to give a concise background on the region, its core varietals and some of the more remarkable labels we've experienced like Opus One, Cade, Grgich Hills, Heitz Cellar, Silver Oak, Stags' Leap and (once-in-a-lifetime) Screaming Eagle. Rather, with its leading reputation and often-exorbitant prices to boot, sourcing product from this region can be a hassle for any property that isn't ultra-high-end. How can you tell what's good and what's only perceived as good because of the Napa naming? How can you stock bottles that are both explosively tasty and quintessentially Californian, but also cost accessible? Lastly, how do you convince guests that the steep bottle price is worth the purchase?

In other words, when approaching NorCal wines, you need a strategy. At the bare minimum, recruit a prudent wine merchant with experience in the region. Let him or her do the initial leg work and make recommendations based upon your unique situation – that is, budget, restaurant classification, average clientele, revenue expectations, cellar conditions and so on. As for convincing patrons of the value in the top-tier bottles, it shouldn't be too hard; the accolades accrued over the past four decades speak for themselves.

Next, even though it may be a tad wallet-emptying on your part, you must start tasting these wines for yourself. They're darn good after all. Try

to distinguish which varietals mesh best with your taste buds and how NorCal wines differ from those made in, say, Italy or France. There is a reason for the 'Big Californian Cab' stereotype and you won't be able to identify its fruit-bursting punch by reading a description off a webpage. Through this (rigorous) trial and error, find a few wineries that you would deem as *easy drinkers* – those that aren't too pricey and can work for a variety of occasions.

Remember, the ultimate role of building your wine list and cellar is profitability. Your wine pricing should reflect and be proportionate to your entrée selling prices. This is what could be deemed as *pricing efficiency* where the most effective sales-to-profit ratio is obtained with more seemingly fair sticker prices and a more approachable selection on the list. True, one or two 'badge' bottles might seem exciting but remember that there are carrying costs on those inventory items that rarely turn, if at all.

Supporting SoCal

As it concerns vinicultural discussion of Southern California, we would include many of the southern-leaning AVAs of the Central Coast north of the seaside town of Santa Barbara as well as the AVAs sandwiched between Los Angeles and San Diego.

Everyone has heard of the Santa Ynez Valley – of *Sideways* fame – but also included in this broad swath of semi-arid valleys are, starting from the north and moving south, Paso Robles, San Luis Obispo, Arroyo Grande, Santa Maria and the Santa Rita Hills, while on the other side of Greater Los Angeles and the Inland Empire you have the burgeoning areas of Temecula as well as San Pasqual Valley and Ramona Valley, both within San Diego County.

Like their northern neighbors, these regions largely utilize the same varietals and growing techniques that have come to be representative of the state's wine production. This means the fruit-forward, oft-jammy, New World reds made primarily from Cabernet Sauvignon, Merlot, Zinfandel and Pinot Noir as well as numerous well-oaked, beyond-buttery Chardonnay and dry, yet brightly acidic Sauvignon Blanc done in the 'Fumé Blanc' style.

What's remarkable about California is that once you look beyond the name recognition of Napa County and Sonoma County, this state still has an uncountable number of gems, especially in SoCal where the growing regions aren't quite as established – both domestically and internationally – as those an hour's drive from San Francisco. In practicality, this means that your dollar goes a bit further when sourcing from these areas, especially when compared to Napa and Sonoma where the average prices of good bottles are now reaching unobtainable levels to most consumers.

Many renowned bottles from NorCal are now garnering so much *sticker stock* that they are turning off customers from purchasing altogether. As the very name of the state carries with it so much inherent prestige and trust in its quality of production, sourcing lesser-known and more reasonably priced wines from SoCal will help to mitigate these types of concerns by offering patrons something that's similar but mildly different and still generously affordable.

Californian wines are all but a requirement for menus these days, at least within a North American context. For many customers, stocking a few vintages from NorCal brings peace of mind that halos back onto the perceived quality of the food. Others deem these prestigious entries as necessary for special occasions. But that doesn't mean you can't still surprise and delight by rounding out your wine list with some niche or esoteric offerings. And so, the Golden State is yours to rediscover.

As a final aside, the elevated demand that has caused winemakers to develop newer areas like Temecula and San Diego County has in part extended in the breezy coastal communities and hot inland hills of Northwest Mexico south of Tijuana in Baja California, offering yet another opportunity to excite your guests with something unexpected. With a climate that's just a touch hotter and drier than the Californian coast, they're starting to produce bottles that are on par with those made in the United States and often done in more of an Old World style.

Cascade Wines

The New World has come a long way over the past few decades. Since the Judgment of Paris in 1976 (as previously mentioned, where a California winery, Chateau Montelena, took top prize), vintners beyond the hallowed soils of the Mediterranean have sought to grow their stocks as far more than jug wine. It is the knowledge and passion for the process of winemaking that gives life to the final product, not just where you are on a map.

North of the Golden State, in Oregon and in Washington, vintners are doing incredible things, and often for a fraction of the cost to consumers when compared to the some of the outrageous price tags on renowned Californian labels. While the AVAs vary wildly across these two territories when it comes to climate, soil and varietals cultivated, the dominant influence is the Cascade Mountains – the spine that runs up the middle of the Northwest and hence the naming of this chapter.

First of note is the Willamette Valley in Oregon, straddling the westward side of the Cascades and sheltered from Pacific tempests by two other minor ranges. Through a combination of ideally suited terroir and dedicated winemaking, this region now produces decent Pinot Gris as well as some of the world's best Pinot Noir – bottles that can go toe-to-toe with anything produced in Burgundy or New Zealand.

Further up the coast it becomes a bit too frigid for proper grapevine maturation. And so, the production migrates to the leeward side of the Cascades in the rain-shadowed Columbia Valley where the high latitude – that is, vastly extended daylight hours during summer – allow for such colder climate varietals like Cabernet Franc, Chardonnay, Gewürztraminer, Riesling and Sauvignon Blanc to thrive. Given its dry summers, however, many vintners have successfully stabilized the production of Cabernet Sauvignon, Merlot and Syrah – traditionally hot climate varietals – so much so that they represent the dominant share of the annual red grape crush.

While these wines have on average lower price tags than their Californian neighbors, this is not a result of poor quality but rather a lack of recognition. To bring these wines to the forefront, you must train your staff accordingly as well as give these wines the spotlight through what may ostensibly be called a varietal noncompete clause.

Consider a scenario where you are planning to put Willamette's raison d'être – Pinot Noir – on the menu. Assume that your average guest is familiar with Burgundy, California and New Zealand but not with the hidden gems of the Northwest. If you also list Pinot Noir from those three other better-known regions, then the Willamette bottle won't stand a chance of garnering significant sales because most patrons will default to what they already know. Instead, if you were to only offer Pinot Noir from Oregon – giving them a choice of, say, two or three wineries – then those guests in search of such a flavor spectrum would have no choice but to try one or at least ask their server to describe it in more detail.

While such a clear noncompete cannot be stated for Washington which has yet to refine its identity down to a single grape or blending style, Syrah represents the best bet. The state's production for this grape is remarkable, with unique characteristics that differentiate the drop from its Australian Shiraz and Côte du Rhône counterparts. As most people are still unacquainted with the pleasures of sampling a Syrah from the Northwest, by putting one on the wine list and not drowning it in a sea of other similarly full-bodied, inky palates, you may find that your customers will be amazed by your recommendation.

A Tale of Two Canadas

We are proudly Canadian. We are proudly Torontonian. Dovetailing our home city's booming growth in the 21st century has been the proliferation of Ontario wine and viticulture, centered around the Niagara Peninsula, but not excluding Prince Edward County to the east of Toronto and other sub-appellations.

As our knowledge increased with each day trip to a vineyard or two, our curiosity for other Canadian appellations grew likewise. One has always stood out – none other than the spectacular Okanagan Valley about five hours' drive east from Vancouver, British Columbia. With Niagara representing the east and the Okanagan representing the west, Canada now has plenty of wines to compete on the world stage.

Both Niagara and the Okanagan Valley are relatively smaller in physical area than other appellations that produce for the world market. As well, Canadian winters make for shorter growing seasons and less overall yield, even though both are geographically tempered by the northern chills for moderately hotter and drier microclimates. On top of all this, our fellow Canucks have developed quite the appetite for this purple elixir, so many of the bottles are consumed locally.

All this means that Canadian vintages may be a tad harder to source than those from other regions. But exclusivity is an allure in its own right. Don't underestimate the quality either. Both regions cater to the international bestselling varietals such as Cabernet Sauvignon, Merlot, Pinot Noir, Chardonnay, Cabernet Franc, Pinot Gris and Sauvignon Blanc. We find that it's especially important to follow a farmer's almanac when choosing your year. This is because the shorter growing season leaves the fruit far more vulnerable to week-over-week fluctuations. For instance, if there's a whopping dose of rain during the tail end of summer (August and September), the acids and sugars cannot concentrate within the grapes, severely affecting flavor.

Despite these concerns, the shorter season has one definite advantage: ice wine. Bar none, Canada has the best ice wines in the world. The most popular base strains include Riesling, Vidal, Gewürztraminer and Cabernet Franc (as well as other red ice wines made from a blend of late harvest grapes). The key with ice wines – and why Canada does them so well – is that the fruit must be left on the vine during the early stages of winter until they solidify to a temperature no warmer than -8ºC (17ºF). This first frost leaves the grapes highly concentrated with sugars, resulting in a sweet beverage with a hefty alcohol percentage. They're outstanding for dessert, but a glass also works as an aperitif or an appetizer accompaniment.

You might initially decide to put a Canadian vintage on the menu out of pure novelty, but rest assured the winemakers here are not beginners. Look over the official stamp of assurance – a gold medallion emblazoned with the letters VQA (Vintners Quality Alliance).

Tasting and Cycling Through Canada's Prince Edward County

International travel restrictions during the pandemic forced all of us to rethink our vacation prospects, and for the two of us this meant researching areas within driving range instead of jet setting off to Asia, Europe or Latin America. Of course, we always try to orient our travels around wine in whatever way possible, so we chose Prince Edward County (PEC) in Ontario, a burgeoning wine region less than three hours from Toronto. Importantly for you, there are important lessons about marketing alcoholic beverages and creating a dining experience, no matter where in the globe you find yourself.

By burgeoning, we mean that PEC has only recently been discovered by Toronto's sizeable yuppie and wealthy retiree communities when compared to the established Niagara Peninsula which brought Canada to the world stage via its ice wines. The former cohort of thirtysomething travelers comes for weekend retreats while the latter is increasingly buying lots and building mansions for year-round occupation. Both are fueling the development of boutique hotels, B&Bs, high-end restaurants and vacation rental properties as well as more conversions of hay pastures into vineyards.

The first lesson from this backstory is that if you can grow wine in Canada of all places then you can grow it just about anywhere with the right knowhow. As such, if you own or work at a rural property, be on the lookout for aspiring wineries within an hour's drive that you can direct guests to for a fun outing.

Even though PEC is still in its youth, that doesn't mean there aren't gems to be found. We fondly remember the Pinot Noir at Norman Hardie Winery, best enjoyed while eating pizza alfresco at the vineyard, made fresh from the outdoor pizza oven in full view while the eponymous winemaker worked the grape sorting machine right next to it. Then across the street you have Casa Dea which is one of the few to try its hand at a tasty Melon de Bourgogne in addition to a full slate of appassimento vintages reminiscent of Amarone. Further along the Taste Trail, as it's called, is Closson Chase with a splendid array of Chardonnay and a beautifully manicured garden perfect for outdoor events. Fourth of note, a tour through PEC isn't complete without a visit to Huff Estates where, beyond its cozy inn and impressive restaurant, the signature attraction is its vast outdoor sculpture gallery.

Ambling about from winery to winery, another prominent thing you'll notice in PEC is the large number of cyclists along the backroads. While this is a common sight for just about any wine region, what's critical is that all the main stops now cater to this audience, with all the hotels, B&Bs and restaurants in the area also following suit with services and amenities to attend to cyclists' specific needs.

Thinking broadly about our description of PEC, do you notice in the above paragraphs how we didn't cite any specific vintages? That's because these aren't the main draws to the region. The takeaway is that it's not just about getting top marks in any international wine ranking; it's about creating an experience for which the beverage is but one component. Review the four vineyards we cited; the common theme is that there's an elevator pitch for each that is broader than one individual vintage.

Say you run a boutique resort embedded within a wine region. So what? This isn't reason enough to command nightly rates above what your comp set is charging. You will always need an x-factor to escape the confines of an apples-to-apples price comparison that most of your prospective customers will be performing during the travel research phase. A dearth of proper guestroom supply in PEC may mean, for the time being, that hoteliers there can rest on their laurels, but if a property wants to grow rate while posting healthy year-round occupancy figures it nonetheless has to make then promote a highly emotional driver for guests. Ditto for restaurants where popularity ebbs and flows; creating lasting appeal requires creating a great experience through a combination of food, beverages, service and ambiance.

The beauty of this principle is that it is ubiquitous and yet it encompasses near-infinite possibilities for those who take the time to craft a veritable USP. Perhaps you create your own outdoor art walk or, with less capex, you decide to be the king of activities available in your local territory. Even though it is an insurmountable part of the dining experience, an exceptional wine list is often not enough for a hotel or restaurant to generate top-of-funnel awareness.

South Africa Comes to the World Stage

After Australia, the penultimate Southern Hemisphere exporter is another former crown colony, South Africa. And as with its Commonwealth counterpart, the nation's winemaking heritage goes together with European colonization.

For starters, sneak a glance at a world map, or recall the nation's location from memory; specifically, the region around the Cape of Good Hope at the southwestern corner of the nation. This area denotes the Cape Peninsula and, more broadly, the Western Cape, including the first Dutch colony, and later the first British colony, that would become the city of

Cape Town. Special to the Cape Peninsula is the intersection of weather systems from the Atlantic Ocean and Indian Ocean currents with a more-than-generous contribution from the Antarctic that acts to drastically temper humidity.

All this, in addition to some prominent mountains, valleys and flatlands amounts to hot, dry, sunlight-heavy summer seasons lasting from November to April, much like the Mediterranean. However, certain growing regions – 'wards' as they are locally termed – experience sizably milder and wetter year-round conditions, especially those closest to the coast. This unique terroir has created many sundry microclimates, and thus, many diverse cultivars.

One part climate, another part topography and a third part colonization, to this day the Western Cape is where the vast majority of South Africa's viticultural activity transpires. The Dutch East India Company was the first to instigate this development, importing grapevines and harvesting the fruit for sailors to fend off scurvy during the passage from Europe to India and Southeast Asia. As you know, wherever there are fecund grapevines, there will soon be winemaking. Indeed, by 1659, a vineyard was established at Constantia just north of Cape Town.

Once the colony was folded into the British Empire, production sharply increased throughout the 19th century to offset the dominant French on the international market. With the bulk of South African wines exported to Great Britain, the nation's industry declined towards the end of the century following the dissolution of the preferential tariffs that precluded French vintages. For most of the 20th century, vintners suffered tremendously under Apartheid as worldwide boycotts thwarted overseas commerce and knowledge exchange.

But with the collapse of this racial segregation system in 1994, South Africa's winemaking quickly rebounded and is now the eighth largest worldwide producer and exporter. Adhering to the purview of the internal Wine of Origin administration, there are now roughly 60 active wards with most of the harvest controlled by several large cooperatives. Alongside this resurgence has come a renewed focus on international prospects as many vineyards have shifted towards the noble varietals of Cabernet Sauvignon, Chardonnay, Merlot, Pinot Noir, Sauvignon Blanc and Shiraz.

However, the reopening of trade routes has also allowed for a revival of South Africa's own cultivars and styles. Most pronounced are the fortified wines designed under the Cape Port marker. Heavily influenced by Portuguese seafarers migrating through the Cape Colony, these spirits cover a wide range of varietals, both white and red, as well as winemaking techniques, comprising a narrow assortment of strict vintage classifications.

Three more atypical grape pedigrees nearing the top of South Africa's production list are Chenin Blanc, Colombard and Pinotage. Chenin Blanc, also called Steen, is originally from the Loire Valley in northwestern France and has been adapted mainly for dry dessert wines and sparkling whites as well as those in the Cape Port vein. Colombard, an offspring of Chenin Blanc, is a sweeter white used mainly for the Cape Port wines. Lastly, Pinotage, a deep red cross of Pinot Noir, was first crafted in the Western Cape and is now a required constituent in blends produced in the region.

Our first morsel of advice is to consider these three varietals popular to South Africa, if only to offer the surface allure of something more exotic. Imagine your wine list already boasting a premier stable of the usual suspects; a label with an unfamiliar base ingredient may be enough to pique the more audacious patron and encourage extra sales.

As for dabbling in the Cape Port style wines, consider getting in touch with a Cape Wine Master, the highest formal qualification within the South African wine industry, to canvass their knowledge and stamp of authenticity. Due to their strengthened nature at or above 16% alcohol content, Cape Port vintages may be more suitable as aperitifs or dessert accompaniments. Save for their extensive local appeal, these fortified wines remain comparatively unknown most elsewhere. Hence, conspicuous labeling or their inclusion in pairing suggestions may be required to point customers in the right direction.

South American Wines

We've chosen to approach the wines of South America as a singular unit; a move not out of any deficiency of viticultural narrative in each country or laziness on our part, but because of their common ancestor – Spain (except for Brazil). The two primary candidates for discussion are Argentina and Chile given their top ten volumes of global production. As such, we will focus on these two nations. However, this does not preclude such other burgeoning and smaller growing regions within Bolivia, Brazil's Rio Grande do Sul, Paraguay, Peru (especially the spirit Pisco) and Uruguay.

Totaled together, Argentina and Chile now make more wine by tonnage than the United States, respectively as the fifth and tenth largest worldwide producers. This was not always the case, however. Both nations were wracked by decades of turbulent governments and economic strife throughout the 20th century. Looking back even further, although colonization was the key spark for the import of grape stocks and grafts in the 16th century, Spanish overseers sought to restrict viticultural farming in the New World to avoid competition with vintners back home.

Nevertheless, wine culture prospered, giving us many unique tastes and stable appellations for which we can now fully reap the savory benefits. Of note, South America largely escaped the phylloxera blight that ruined vineyards throughout Europe in the 19th century. This devastation caused many French, Italian and Spanish winemakers to emigrate to Argentina and Chile, bringing with them their varietals and wisdom. But most of the production during this period was still devoted to table grapes and jug wine for local consumption.

It wasn't until the turn into the 21st century that South America really took to the world stage with a gallant desire to compete at the international level. For this, vineyards hired flying winemakers throughout the 1990s and 2000s to elevate the quality of wines to modern standards of export set for large buying countries like Great Britain, United States and, more recently China, as well as a greater replanting and focus on the more pervasive commercial mainstays.

Nowadays, South American wines are widely considered New World in their taste spectrums, particularly the whites. But there are some peculiarities about them that can prop your wine list up with that extra slice of fascination. Namely, the early grafters didn't properly control their varietal lineage and as such some obvious mislabeling has occurred. No matter, the ampelographers are on the case.

Proceeding in alphabetical order with Argentina, what is most apparent about Argentine wines is that the vast majority of export quality production takes places in Mendoza and its neighboring province of San Juan in the Andean foothills. This high altitude, semi-arid cordillera environment, with its hot summers and sharp nighttime temperature drops, elicits softer flavors with bolder tannins in the reds. It's no wonder that Malbec is now the grape of choice, and you would be hard-pressed to find an area elsewhere in the world that does this varietal better.

Moreover, reds account for over 60% of wine exports with other key varietals including Cabernet Sauvignon, Syrah and Tempranillo. Worth noting is the Italian Charbono strain, locally known as Bonarda, which was almost completely extricated from European fields by the phylloxera epidemic. Surviving in Argentina, it is now a flavorful runner up in popularity to the Malbec. Given its blackened skins, Charbono is somewhat counterintuitive as the wine has a deep empurpled color yet a fruity, acidic profile.

An important postscript for the Argentine Malbec, they've been bred more towards the tart flavors of Cabernet Sauvignon and less like the conventional Malbec which belies a sugary plum and cherry taste. To bolster this dissimilarity, it's rather common to find Malbec as the major grape in a mix that includes Cabernet Sauvignon, Syrah and Petit Verdot, in turn creating a diverse array of wines to choose from.

On the white front, Argentine exports have adopted the international cornerstones of Sauvignon Blanc, Chardonnay, Pinot Gris, Riesling, Sémillon and Viognier while the jug wine varietal of Pedro Giménez continues to decline. From personal experience, if you plan to dabble with Argentine alcohol, stick with the reds and the most perfected of the lot, Malbec and Bonarda; the former for a solid expression of a familiar grape and the latter for something a tad more exotic and intrepid.

As for Chile, any agronomical discussion should include a brief overview of the country's svelte, latitude-crossing geographic borders along with the inescapable presence of the towering Andes. Together, these two have caused most of the premier Chilean flights to aggregate within the 800-mile stretch between the 32nd and 38th parallels centered on the capital, Santiago, where the climate most imitates that of the Mediterranean. The mild Pacific currents along with the rain shadow protection induced by the Andes and the coastal range provide vineyards with some of the most stable growing conditions in the world. Minimal weather fluctuations mean consistent vintages – a boon for rolling purchase orders.

Much like how Argentina has the Malbec, Chile has the Merlot, for which the country's harvest rivals the renowned incumbents in California and France. Chile also favors Cabernet Sauvignon, although their produce leans toward a softer palate akin to a proper Cab-Merlot blend. Third in the reds, and contributing towards many of the country's taste discrepancies, is the Carménère grape which, like Charbono in Argentina, was largely destroyed by the phylloxera scourge only to live on in the New World.

Carménère, with its archetypal rubicund coloration and rich, mellow profile, has largely been incorrectly labeled as Merlot. Now that more professional vintners are active, this once popular French varietal is back in vogue nearly 150 years after its disappearance from Europe. The lost grape is recognized as a distinct lure for the country's wines, restored to its own pedigree separate from Merlot as well as thriving as a near-exclusive blending ingredient in Chilean mainstays.

These same mistaken identity cases apply to many Sauvignon Blanc vineyards where the parent stocks have been found to be of Sauvignonasse and Sémillon descent, affording many Chilean whites with softer, floral notes instead of the quintessential fruitiness of other Sauvignon Blanc flights from the New World. Whatever the case, the top four picks of Cabernet Sauvignon, Carménère, Merlot and Sauvignon Blanc will add some variety and perhaps a few interesting conversations to your wine list.

Wines from Down Under

When autumn comes to the Northern Hemisphere, it's time to turn your oenophilic gaze on our southern neighborhoods where things are literally heating up. Chief amongst the southern producers is Australia; a country and a continent, as well as the world's seventh largest wine producer and, remarkably, now the world's fourth largest wine exporter.

The Aussie wine story is peculiar as the ecosystem had no native grape stocks prior to the British infusion beginning around the early 19th century. Even then, the continent's climate is widely erratic, capable of going from drought to flood and back all within a single decade – not the best for cementing cultivars and motivating financiers. (Nota bene: starting a vineyard capable of export quantities typically requires millions of dollars upfront.)

So it was that for the longest time, the semi-arid valleys and grasslands (Australia is also the flattest continent by the way) of Victoria, New South

Wales, South Australia and Western Australia (four of the nation's now prominent wine-producing states) were reserved for shepherds, farmers and miners. That's not to say that winemaking was absent, but still an oddity.

Things started to change in the late 1950s. Primarily, science had bolstered the root stocks to better suit the unstable Aussie weather conditions and resist a certain sinister pest, and worldwide population booms warranted a greater supply. The industry reached a fever pitch in the mid-1990s as corporations swooped in with their economies of scale and marketing savvy to more formally debut Australian wines to the world market. The country hasn't looked back since, and indeed the grapevine business remains one of the country's largest growth sectors.

As for the wines themselves, they may not hold the longstanding barreling traditions and prestige of vineyards in France and Italy, but that would be a naïve pretense to belittle the Australians' rich and complex flavors. Borrowing chiefly from the most popular Old World varietals – Chardonnay, Pinot Noir, Riesling, Sauvignon Blanc, Merlot and Cabernet Sauvignon – these wines are quintessentially New World. Brightly acidic with pungent sugars, the reds are rarely heavy, and the whites never fail to dance on the palate. Given this archetypal taste profile, the nation's stable of wines is perfect for plugging the gaps on your menu where a flighty, fruity elixir is required.

Our hunch is to start with the more established and bountiful producing regions including the Margaret River south of Perth, Hunter Valley and Mudgee, about four hours inland from Sydney and the Yarra River Valley outside of Melbourne. But none compared to the rolling hills surrounding Adelaide in South Australia (Barossa Valley, Coonawarra, Eden Plains, McLaren Vale and the Riverland), home to the Southern Hemisphere's largest wineries and most of the country's viticultural heritage.

Wines are a matter of *taste and you shall receive*. Given its bourgeois and still largely experimental character, Australian labels are completely winemaker-dependent (aren't they all?). Use a buyer's guide or an expert wine merchant to select a few renowned bottles for initial sampling. As well, Aussie vintners generally keep an impressive cohort at any major tasting convention, so attendance to one of these events can earn you a meeting to learn more firsthand.

What's best is the price. Never outrageously marked up, the nation's bottles are generally very reasonable for the average patron and are ready to drink at a young age. Vintage is less of a concern, as their wines typically remain consistent year to year.

A New Zealand Nosh

Viticulture in this small, remote, agrarian nation was less so a matter of naturally suitable terroir and more so happenstance. When the Brits ended their exclusive trade agreements for New Zealand meat and dairy products in 1973, it left quite a few Kiwis scrambling for creative ways to stay solvent.

If there's a will, there's a way, especially when alcohol is involved. In under a decade, clever farmers had successfully adapted Sauvignon Blanc to select, rain-shadowed pockets on both the North and South Islands. Sandwiched by the Coral Sea and the Pacific Ocean, New Zealand has a maritime climate, imbuing its grapes with different flavors. Specifically, the persistent wetness and cool summer nights result in less sugar concentration and lower acidity.

Within 50 years, New Zealand has emerged to rival many other producing nations, both in quantity and quality. While the country is still experimenting and diversifying the varietals it grows, when it comes to presenting the average customer with a Kiwi Vino-USP, we are essentially talking about Sauvignon Blanc and Pinot Noir from the Marlborough region near the northern tip of the South Island, accounting for over three-quarters of the country's production.

What we've found is that these two varietals along with the third most common, Chardonnay, are all consistently delicious and reasonably priced. We've long been a fan of New Zealand wines, but it wasn't until last spring when we had the opportunity to sample them in full during our first sojourn to Auckland.

Our suggestion for you as a budding oenophile is to taste-test Kiwi Pinot Noir and Sauvignon Blanc against their counterparts from other premier growing regions. Match a New Zealand Pinot against one from NorCal and Burgundy and you'll find that the lower acidity is immediately palatable, with the Kiwi bottles further distinguished by their earthy, savory and full-bodied notes.

For the whites, many already consider New Zealand Sauvignon Blanc to be the best in the world of this varietal, but it is nevertheless worthwhile to compare a drop or two with those produced in the Loire Valley or, if you are in the mood, Chile, South Australia, the Western Cape and Ontario. For quintessential Kiwi Sauvignon Blanc, most labels are light on the tongue with clean notes of tropical fruit and melon – ideal for salads, white fish or wine newcomers. They also tend to be aged in steel casks, adding to their feathery taste.

While the island nation undoubtedly has a lot more to offer than this one growing region and two varietals, the purpose here is, as always, to help you enhance wine sales and meal satisfaction with simplicity often the best route, particularly when labor is already pressed for time and supply chains on lesser-known bottles can be erratic. For this, it's best to present customers with only a few, well-distinguished options. Hence, supplementing your list with a New Zealand Pinot Noir is a great alternative to the French or Californian equivalents while a Kiwi Sauvignon Blanc is always a versatile addition.

What About China?

Through our wine studies, one curiosity we've stumbled upon pertains to China. The nation of over 1.4 billion people and rapidly proliferating wealth is starting to consume a lot of wine. Not only that, but China currently stands as the fifth biggest grape producer in the world (most for internal consumption), and yet they are still only in the infant stages of developing their own internal haughty viticulture and prize-worthy vintners.

In terms of per capita statistics (attained for 2019 for pre-pandemic numbers), China currently rests far down the list at roughly 0.15 liters per person per year. Although this ratio pales in comparison to countries where wine is life, when it comes to China you always must consider the sheer scale of the country. For some of the heaviest drinkers, France's population sits at 67 million, Italy at 60 million and Portugal at 10 million. China has 1.4 billion people; approximately ten times that of France, Italy and Portugal combined. If wine culture catches on in China, even by just a little bit, we are talking colossal increases of consumption across all price points.

And this is already happening. China has grown quite the voracious appetite for imports, chiefly from prestigious winemakers in France, Italy, Germany and the United States. Think the big, eminent châteaux: Pétrus, Cheval Blanc, Mouton Rothschild and the classic Burgundies like Romanée-Conti. These name examples are just for France, but if you know these bottles then you know the caliber we are talking about.

The continued presence of a gigantic fine wine buyer and consumer like China suggests, through straightforward supply and demand, that worldwide prices are bound to increase, especially at the upper end of the market which is being yanked into the stratosphere. If you're scouting for evidence of this budding trend, look no further than Sotheby's with its Hong Kong location reaping huge rewards from this incredible rise in Chinese demand.

On an individual property basis, these sorts of macroeconomic analyses will probably have little impact in the short run, especially since this gross inflation affects Chinese domestic prices more so than wholesale elsewhere in the world. Just don't be surprised that the lurking aftershock of China's heightened consumption causes the entire market to float upwards as well. We say lurking because it will be a slow, years-long effect, but it will nevertheless impact your bottom line.

Perhaps now is the right time to explore the bevy of new growers and regions reaching maturity? These are factors which are simultaneously acting to buffer the supply side of things and, from their perspective, capitalize on the mounting worldwide demand. Moreover, given the abundance of flying winemakers and knowledge sharing via the internet, it is now easier for a grape producer or vintner to perfect their technique in a shorter time span.

With this China's increasing affluence also comes more outbound travel (COVID-19 lockdowns aside) and more expendable cash for such luxury items as top-tier alcoholic beverages while traveling. What libations are popular with Chinese patrons? Are their actions abroad akin to what they would purchase at home? And more specifically, how can you better appeal to Chinese guests through a more engaging wine list?

There are many other alcoholic beverages that compete with wine for top esteem in mainland China – mainly beer (Tsingtao being both popular and flavorful), Baijiu, Maotai, whiskey, Brandy and rice liquors. Stocking just one of these mainstays might help to ease incomers from Chinese by giving them a stronger sense of home when visiting a foreign land, thus formulating better impressions of your hotel. To give you some perspective, imagine you are traveling in China, and with so many unfamiliar food choices wouldn't it be somewhat calming to get a burger or a pizza once in a while?

Recent polls show that China's appetite for foreign wine mostly extends to reds. Our first suggestion is therefore to ensure that your wine list has a robust selection of reds from wine-producing nations known to be at the top of their game (in the same vein as those abovementioned). This may seem prejudiced against white wines, but it's simply where the demand presently is. Plus, through our many red-versus-white arguments in the past, the consensus is always that red pairs better with more meals, especially those with a meat or poultry main and a rich sauce.

From a purchaser's perspective, China's homegrown wineries are still too far in their adolescence for us to recommend a hearty investment for your cellars. Right now, a Chinese wine on the menu is likely to be chosen more out of novelty than out of quality. But as is the case with nearly every other industry, this booming nation is rife with fast learners and hard workers, so expect their producing regions to be making an increasingly significant impact on the world stage as the grapevines and vintners reach maturity over the next two decades.

It's important to also remember that like any other cosmopolitan jetsetter, Chinese travelers are looking to live the new and experience the unknown. Give them an authentic localized experience through your wine list and pairing choices, and you will undoubtedly see a strong appreciation for your efforts. As well, offering one or two liquor options that are cross-pleasers – those that appeal to Chinese consumers as well as those from another large demographic – may work better than narrowcast attractors.

LOVE EVERY REGION

Simplify and Summarize

We've covered many of the key wine growing regions. Now is a good time to reflect on the many of options for you to consider in building your wine strategy. That is, once you begin to truly engross yourself in viticulture, you'll start to relish and indeed love all the details that distinguish the subtle characteristics of one bottle from another.

Once you deepen your knowledge of all things related to this cosmopolitan libation, you'll realize that wine is as much about what's in the bottle (varietal, production methods, vintage) and where bottle came from (terroir, climate, yearly weather variations) as it is the people who made it. As such, it's important to have a few anecdotes handy about all three sides of this equation to further develop the narrative for a customer no matter which way they lean.

Communicating that you or your servers love wine to enrich a patron's dining experience means having that USP – the elevator pitch – ready for each label on the menu to quickly convey the most pertinent details. Below are some of those USPs – a cheat sheet if you will – as an exercise to get you in the habit of simplifying your communications to help your servers enhance wine sales.

And as a final note, one other thing you will realize as you deepen your regional proficiency is that the more you learn about wine, the less you actually know. Every grapevine, vineyard or winery is slightly different and constantly evolving. This is one of the remarkable beauties of wine and what makes it a lifelong obsession.

Australia: Known for its Shiraz, a bastardized naming of the Southern French grape of Syrah, this New World producer has plenty to offer in the mid and mid-upper tiers, with many of its wines emulating the Californian style in production and flavor.

Austria: Although this landlocked nation has plenty to offer, its foremost gift to the world is the Grüner Veltliner, a tart greenish-hued white with distinct notes of crisp apple.

Bordeaux: A vast and highly admired region in the southwest of France, it's most prestigious châteaux use a red blend of Cabernet Sauvignon,

Merlot, Cabernet Franc and Petit Verdot, the proportions of which depend on whether the vineyard is situated on the Left Bank (south side) or the Right Bank (north side) of the region's two main rivers. Bottles from the five premier cru houses easily run over a thousand dollars.

Burgundy: Light, crisp Pinot Noir for reds and complex, slightly chalky Chardonnay for whites. Look for grand cru or premier cru labels to indicate the best in the world in these two varietals.

Canada: A vast nation that, for winemaking, can be whittled down to the Okanagan Valley in British Columbia as well as both the Niagara Peninsula and Prince Edward County in Ontario. Harnessing the harsh northern climate, Canada is best known for its ice wines, a delightful and syrupy addition to any dessert.

Eastern Europe: Lots of hidden gems are now coming out of the Balkan states, Hungary, Romania, Bulgaria, and, to a lesser extent, Moldova and parts of Russia, while the Tokaj region in Hungary will always be known for exquisite dessert wines.

Germany: Coming into its own of late, the steep vineyards along the Rhine are where vintners have perfected the nation's white wine centerpiece – Riesling – while the Spätburgunder and Dornfelder varietals make for rich yet breezy reds.

Greece: With a vinicultural legacy dating farther back than the written word, Greece's wines are as diverse as its many Aegean Islands, all of them delivering strong Old World flavors. If you want to know names, remember Assyrtiko for white and Xinomavro for red.

Loire Valley: A northwestern-facing region in France, its wines are expressive of its colder climate with crisp, light Sauvignon Blanc and Cabernet Franc.

New Zealand: The cooler oceanic climate makes for the perfect environment for Sauvignon Blanc and Pinot Noir, most hailing from Marlborough, a hot pocket on the northern shores of South Island.

Northern California: The prestigious appellations of Napa and Sonoma Counties ostensibly produce the quintessential New World flavor of fresh, bursting fruit and complex sugars in its Cabernet Sauvignon, Zinfandel and buttery Chardonnay offerings.

Pacific Cascades: A broad grouping for all wines made in the states of Oregon and Washington, highlights include Pinot Noir from the Willamette Valley and Syrah from the leeward side of the Cascade Mountains.

Piedmont: The sweltering summers and milder winters in Northwest Italy help to create some of the most impressive wines in the world with the best hills saved for Barolo or Barbaresco, yet everyday drinkers like Nebbiolo or the ultra-sweet Moscato d'Asti also have their moments.

Portugal: Having developed their own varietals long ago, this Atlantic country has some great drops, primarily from the banks of the Douro River where the fortified port wines are also made.

South Africa: The lands around Cape Town are ideal for winemaking and, even though the past two decades have been a shift towards international varietals, the country's best are still its homegrown hybrids – Pinotage for red, and Colombard and Steen for white.

South America: Argentina ostensibly makes stronger, drier and spicier Malbec than Southern France where the grape originates, while Chile has rediscovered the lost Carménère varietal which produces a deep crimson wine bursting with softer flavors of red fruit.

Southern California: From the Central Coast and the hallowed Santa Ynez Valley through to the burgeoning pockets of production north of San Diego, there are countless hidden gems to be found in the reaches below the glorified Napa and Sonoma.

Spain: One of the globe's largest producers and consumers, its hot Iberian growing regions are perfect for leathery, tannic varietals such as Tempranillo. And never forget that Sangria is another summer classic that traditionally uses red as its base.

Tuscany: The most familiar growing region in Italy, your first thought is likely one of Chianti or Brunello di Montalcino, both crafted from the tart and cherry red Sangiovese grape, although never discount the exuberant and experimental Super Tuscans.

Veneto: Italy's largest production area by volume, the Valpolicella wineries in the foothills of the Alps can fit every need while the nectarlike, high-proof Amarone is as unique as they come.

Go on a Tour!

Can you sell wine without ever having visited a winery or vineyard? Sure, it's done all the time. Plus, with the internet at your disposal, you can find out plenty more than is necessary to do the deed. But will you sell wine better and more often if you've become personally acquainted with its production? We assure you: yes.

The more information you know about wine and the greater your personal connection to it, the more your passion for wine will be communicated to customers, both verbally and tonally. It helps put a moving narrative behind the sales pitch. For instance, a guest points to the menu and asks, "Is this Merlot any good?" The waiter may reply with a simple affirmation, which isn't all that encouraging, or instead they could say, "Yes! Our manager toured that winery last summer and he specifically chose that bottle because it was exceptionally smooth and had a rich berry aftertaste you just don't find in other Merlots."

This not only adds credibility to the endorsement but also enriches the waiter's rapport with the patron. Think larger tips which translate into better team morale, but also consider that a congenial rapport will make a guest more lenient towards any perceived service errors. Not that you should have any fumbles in the first place, but with a healthy rapport a patron will be more open to pointing out the shortcoming and inclined to criticize without resentment. You're friends now, after all. This rapport-building also trickles down into better TripAdvisor and Yelp reviews.

Outside of viewing this from a guest's perspective, going on a wine tour is a great team-building exercise. It's your chance to get out of the office and have some fun. Seeing the grapes and wine firsthand as well as experiencing a variety of flavors all at once is a highly educational experience. And direct observational knowledge is remembered far better than any sales factsheet regurgitation.

Furthermore, a tour is an opportunity to discover new wineries in your region and develop relationships with the vintners far and above what email tag will do for you – relationships that may pay off in terms of better deals and first dibs on upcoming releases. To heighten the fun factor and to be as safe as possible, rent a bus so you can all stick together and not have to worry about designated drivers.

Aside from the cost of the outing, the primary consideration is whether you are in the vicinity of a wine-producing region to make for an adequate day trip. Don't panic. You still have options. For one, you'd be hard-pressed to find a major city that doesn't tout an annual wine tasting event, show or festival. Better yet, court a vintner to send reps to your property for an in-house experience. Either way, it's all about attaining that direct knowledge to substantiate recommendations to guests. And the wine tour concept and its benefits can easily be extended to any other supplier, be it a local brewery, distillery, bakery or cheesemaker tour. It's all about injecting a vivid narrative into the menu which translates into a better dining experience.

BEER AND SPIRITS

Aperitif or Digestif?

While some call this the afterwork, mandatory pre-dinner throat and brain lubricant, the French and Italians were kind enough to bestow us with a more elegant term – the aperitif and aperitivo, respectively. For symmetry's sake, they also gave us a word for its after-dinner counterpart – the digestif or digestivo. Understanding some of the nuances with selling the before and after components can help to get more dollars per cover.

Let's start with some simple questions. How many of your guests know what these two words mean and can differentiate between them? How does a restaurant visually demarcate the two (for instance, separate aperitif or cocktail and dessert menus)? And lastly, how are you encouraging patrons to buy drinks specifically for before or after the meal?

To answer these three questions and to connect them with our two Romance language conversions, what we are talking about are *nudges* – those inconspicuous and innocuous suggestions that have a remarkable influence on our behavior.

Don't think of pink polar bears. You've probably heard this one before as it's such a great example. By simply planting the idea of an oddly colored ursine, you are much more likely to dwell on it for a moment or to picture one in your head. This psychological trick jogs the memory because the contrast is unexpected, in turn disrupting our normal brain routines.

What nudges can we give our guests so that they imbibe a bit more beyond what's ordered during the meal itself? Many of the basic tactics are already perfunctory to our industry – separate drink menus left out on the table during the meal and regular server prompts are two that come to mind. Mealtime pacing is also standard, where servers should be trained to ask if a table wants to consider something prior to looking at the food menus. Brevity also works; if the aperitif and pre-dinner cocktail list is kept short, then making a snap decision right at a group is getting settled is much easier. All are proven effective.

Understanding that nudges are almost a form of subterfuge can help us augment these tactics and offer a few extensions. For instance, the art is in how the server prompts your patrons about their hopefully forthcoming libations. Instead of asking a consumer, "Have you decided on drinks?" lead with something softer like, "Have you had a chance to look at the drink menu?"

The first question requires a monetary decision to be made; the customer should read through his or her drink options and make an actual choice. When you add pressure to a sale, the more likely the outcome is to be rejection. The second question only stipulates that said patron browse through the drink list. How hard is that? Then, by browsing and touching the menu (applicable only if QR codes aren't in use), it's recruiting the brain and subconsciously leaning it towards the possibility of a purchase.

Sly but effective, the word 'consider' is softer than 'order'. Obviously, there are those consumers who already have their alcohol agenda preformed before being seated, but for those who are on the fence about ordering an aperitif or any meal accompaniment, subtle shifts like this may be all that's needed.

The other key area to improve has to do with timing. People come to restaurants because they are hungry! This means that from the moment they sit down, getting food is more likely to be of a higher priority than getting drinks, especially if they are famished from work. Hence, you should start them off on the right foot before they jam their heads into the food portion of the menu. Ask guests right as they are being seated if you can start them off with a 'quick' drink (yes, the adjective is important here). Moreover, drink menus should be readily available on the table and in fact more readily available than the food menus, lest guests succumb to the will of their stomachs.

Alas, the French have come to the rescue yet again. Aperitif is used mostly to describe beverages, but it also can refer to little morsels of food to begin the digestive process. If this morsel is complimentary, then it would be called an *amuse bouche*.

If most people when entering a restaurant first and foremost strive to satiate their hunger, then would an amuse bouche work reasonably as a nudge to induce more beverage sales? The idea is that with the stomach temporarily mollified, the brain isn't distracted from pondering cocktail choices.

Next, how would your beverage sales be affected if you were to seat diners and immediately put a basket of fresh bread and a drink list (but no food menus) in front of them? While breadbaskets are waning somewhat of recent, this traditional gratis offering can serve multiple purposes – welcoming the group to set the pace for a great dining experience, whetting the appetite, alleviating immediate hunger pangs so the table is more receptive to patiently drinking before going to appetizers or mains and possibly adding to the memorability of it all through exquisite snacks prepared in-house or at a local bakery.

All this, though, is shunning the after-meal libations. The primary trick here is to ask and you shall (sometimes) receive. If your servers make similarly clever inquiries about drinks at this juncture as they would when first seating their customers, the results will be markedly improved. Another good nudge is to plant the seed of a digestif before the meal or before clearing the plates, either by asking outright or by leaving dessert menus on the table. This works because by the time the mains have been consumed, your patrons have already started to think about heading home; you must prompt them to think differently before this mindset takes hold.

Scoured Grapes

Distilled grape spirits present yet another opportunity for you to boost beverage revenues, both through their gracing of the drinks list and as worthwhile cooking ingredients or pairings for cuisine.

The title here of 'scoured' was a shaky attempt at rhyming off the common 'sour grapes' expression, but in a lot of ways it's still relevant. To scour is to clean – albeit primarily through scrubbing – which is in many ways akin to the process of distilling the alcohol from a fermentation batch of whatever fruit or sugar-filled primary ingredient a producer starts with. After all, they are called 'spirits' because these distilled products are first the hollow, tasteless essence of their juice before additional flavors are reintroduced through barrel aging or other additive processes.

The rough threshold of 20% ABV is important to properly distinguish high-proof liquors from fortified wines such as Marsala, Madeira, Sherry and Vermouth. While you can craft a distilled spirit from almost any fruit or sugar-laden substance, the grape-based beverages offer enough variety to merit their own discussion. These include, but are not limited to, Brandy, Cognac, Armagnac, Grappa, Amaro (sometimes made from grapes), Grand Marnier, Pisco, Tsipouro, Marc, Rakia and Orujo.

When it comes to putting these on the cocktail menu, first note that your outlet patrons may not be readily familiar with any or all these names, which would translate into hesitation or resistance to ordering them straight up. Simply expressing to customers that they are made from grapes and have an amenable flavor may be enough to dispel any friction. Tasting notes written on the menu can work in a similar fashion. For others that need a bit more convincing, a server may explain how they make for superb aperitifs and digestifs, helping to quell the stomach while it macerates the recent meal.

In this sense, such spirits are versatile for every season and can help distinguish your drink list from the prevailing obsessions with artisanal whiskeys, tequilas and mezcal. A personal winter favorite of ours is cognac with a splash of amaretto heated up, while Brandy also goes surprisingly well mixed into hot chocolate. These liquors are adaptable to nearly any cocktail your culinary team might devise; many of the classics you're undoubtedly already familiar with.

As for the food side of things, with many of these imparting hints of vanilla or smoke on top of the more prominent notes of wine, red fruit and aromatic spices added to the mix, the pairings work best with sweets such as fresh fruits, dried fruits, tortes, select pastries like petit fours, chocolates, cream-based desserts, nuts and some cheeses.

The other aspect to this is in using these liquors for cooking, either as a minor component in finishing sauces and soups or as a fiery additive to the pan to bestow a caramelized flavor that's near inimitable from other sources. To understand this in detail, it's important to read up on the *Maillard reaction*. The addition of a spirit or liquor is doubly true for desserts where a bit of alcohol can do wonders to balance out the hyper-sugariness of most last course treats. In any case, all boozy contributions are worth mentioning as ingredients on the menu to present your dishes as more elaborate in their preparation, thereby motivating sales and higher prices.

Whether it's for food or just for the bar, these beverages are yet another chance for you to distinguish your operations and attain culinary leadership within your locale. Challenge your team as a wide assortment of distilled grape spirits – known or niche – may be exactly what you need to help distinguish your restaurant.

A Knack for Cognac

Each country has a proud tradition of turning leftover lemons into boozy lemonade, but perhaps the pinnacle of these is Cognac, and knowing more about this liquor will help you to sell practically any aperitif or digestif.

Much like how Champagne comes exclusively from Champagne, Cognac is eponymously named after the French enclave where it is made. And analogous to Bourbon from Kentucky, that geographic stamp of authenticity – in France's case, an AOC designation – must be continuously earned by strictly adhering to the rules. The varietal of region that's used for Cognac is Ugni Blanc, more commonly known as Trebbiano in Italy, which by the French adjective indicates that it's a white. Then production is specified to be two distillations in copper stills followed by at least two years of aging in French Limousin or Tronçais oak.

Knowing that the English word 'brand' shares a root with the word 'burn', it's a tad ironic that we should learn about effective marketing from this distinctive type of 'Brandy'.

Beyond the rules for production, to further promulgate Cognac's reputation and demand, the commune of Cognac is divided into several subregions, each vying to add dollars to the list price through alluring adjectives. Perhaps the two most distinguished subregions are Grande Champagne and Petite Champagne which, when blended, allow producers to mark the final product as Fine Champagne Cognac so that the other even-more-famous French sparkling wine can be associated with this distilled spirit to help with sales.

The next big step for elevating the sticker price is the grading system based upon the aging of the final bottled product in terms of post-distillation years in the cask.

- *VS (Very Special):* at least two years
- *VSOP (Very Special Old Pale):* at least four years
- *Napoleon:* at least six years
- *XO (Extra Old):* at least a decade

For Cognac and any other barrel-aged alcohol, the main selling point is that more aging imparts more flavor, but distillers also must account for product loss. Wood casks are ever-so-slightly porous, with roughly 3% of volume evaporating each year. This can increase ABV, but the trade-off is that there's less physical liquid to sell.

Typically, a master taster or blender will mix from several casks from different regions to create the flavour unique to that label. This results in hundreds of different products, for which the most popular are the big five of Courvoisier, Hennessy, Martell, Otard and Remy Martin.

Beyond supplying a familiar brand, you can enrich the narrative for patrons at a restaurant or hotel lobby bar by discussing the unique blend of different casks and aging processes used by distillers. The selling is typically reserved for the after-dinner experience as a digestif, dessert accompaniment or nightcap. In the old days, Cognac was the beverage of choice for cigar smokers and, while the tobacco has gone away, this spirit is still around as a time-honored way to finish off a meal.

And to cap off this chapter, let's touch upon the crème de la crème for Cognac – Louis XIII. Produced by Remy Martin, the name honors the first monarch to officially recognize Cognac as its own classification distinct from Armagnac which happens to be the oldest Brandy recorded to be distilled in the world.

Louis XIII is all the rage right now, accomplished largely through exceptional marketing. Made from grapes produced in Grande Champagne vineyards in the immediate southeast of the town of Cognac, the final blend comprises cask-aged distillations ranging from 40 to 100 years old. But the main attraction is the opulent, and a tad garish, handmade crystal decanter, with its studded glass replica of a flask serving as a preeminent symbol of luxury, quality and status.

Outrageously expensive for the everyday drinker, customers should anticipate paying hundreds of dollars for a once-in-a-lifetime, single-ounce taste. For you as the merchant, stocking this particular Cognac, besides its sizeable carrying cost, can by itself act to elevate the restaurant's prestige in order to attract wealthier clientele. Plus, it can anchor the rest of the menu's pricing to help sell more of the other cognacs you have stocked. Ultimately, Cognac is yet one more way to round out a great beverage strategy with lots of opportunities to enhance the dining experience for your guests.

Microbreweries

While this book is primarily about wine, we want to address the growing microbrewery trend as a means of complementing and augmenting your wine list. And for those that aren't in the know, by microbrewery, we're referring to a small, craft beer-making company that produces less than 15,000 barrels per year. There are even hobbyist nanobreweries that produce less than 100 barrels and do it because the brewers like the process.

The concept of the micro or local brewery has existed for thousands of years, proliferating since the libation's invention in ancient Egypt and Mesopotamia right through to medieval times. However, the beverage was always considered more of a thirst quencher than a taste tester, often consumed as 'small beer' by watering it down for all-day consumption.

Then came pasteurization, big national brands, imports and, ultimately, very limited options. Until recently, beer has never really been a mark of sophistication like wine. And to discover the alchemic and urbane subtleties of strange barley and hop combinations, you will have to travel to regions of Ireland, Belgium, Holland, Germany or the Czech Republic.

Much like how everything else has changed in our interconnected world, so too has the beer industry. The internet has played a big role in shattering the entry barriers for brewing. Keen brewers can instantly share recipes and techniques as well as find new ingredient sources and channels for distribution. Microbreweries are also a more realistic startup venture versus wineries or vineyards, requiring far less land, labor and production time. Plus, a microbrewery is hardly dependent on erratic weather conditions, operating indoors and year-round. These factors aside, microbrews still only account for less than 10% of total domestic consumption (in the United States), but they are growing at a staggering rate relative to their mass-marketed counterparts.

Using mainstays as an example, your restaurant's beer choices could include the Budweiser, Coors and Miller varieties, or you could proffer something more eclectic. This is no insult to these major brands' quality, but they are all so commonplace that they have become boring. There's no excitement, no mystery, no sense of discovery. True, some people may only be in the mood for a good old-fashioned Bud Light. But would they be entirely opposed to a craft brew, especially if no major brands were on the menu?

Specialty drafts give you the chance to revitalize your menu with a little adventure and flair. It's no longer just an ale, but a bitter yet smooth malt with floral hop aromas then topped off with a bold, refreshing finish of honey, coffee and almonds. Does this remind you of any other beverage descriptions? Oftentimes, the wine list is given the full attention of the team, while the beer list suffers from neglect.

There are pale ales, lagers, pilsners, honey browns, red ales, amber ales, blondes, wheat beers, session ales, dark beers, porters, stouts, Trappist Ales and plenty of other more obscure flavors. Much like the underlying function of your wine list, your beer choices should serve to augment your overall food experience. Just as there's a vintage to satisfy every person's taste and to pair with each meal, craft beers have already moved in the same direction. Having to explain such options will take up a larger chunk of a waiter's time and perhaps temporarily boggle a customer. Framing this positively, it's a chance for the waiter to establish rapport with a curious patron and thus increase the perceived service level. And just for trivia's sake, a beer sommelier is named a *cicerone.*

Microbrews are also an excellent way to support your local constituency. Your outlet might be located in or near a wine-producing region but, as is more often the case, it is not. Breweries are essentially modified warehouses and can be situated practically anywhere.

Now we're not suggesting that you turn your restaurant or lobby bar into a brewpub. We're merely proposing this yet another potentially unrealized point of differentiation. Fun and interesting beverage options can add to a guest's dining experience and therefore improve the quality of their stay. Plus, such craft beers are also a chance for additional beverage sales as people will be more inclined to have an extra pint of something new or foreign. Along these lines, you could also offer a flight of beers to boost the experiential factor.

Are You a Cider Provider?

Ever since humankind discovered that the sugars in any fruit juice can be fermented to generate enough alcohol to ward off dysentery (a common side effect of drinking water way back in the day), we've been tinkering and experimenting to conjure up ever-tastier beverages. Wine from grapes is the most popular, but we also have such delightful libations as blueberry wine, raspberry ice wine, gin from juniper berries, Schnapps, Brandy, Sherry, Perry from pears and a whole rainbow of liqueurs. Then there's cider, made from apples and especially popular in the United Kingdom, other Commonwealth nations, Germany (where it is called Apfelwein), Ireland and the United States.

It's this last territory which fascinates us the most as the United States has a total population greater than all the others combined and its cider sales are currently on a sharp uptick. You might as well ride this newfound popularity all the way to the piggybank.

Interestingly, cider used to be the bee's knees in America with annual production and consumption easily dwarfing that of beer. But then they passed the idiotic Volstead Act in January 1920 and thousands of acres of apple orchards were burned to the ground to snuff out the 'demonic spread of rampant alcoholism'. Those apple growers who were left were convinced purely by economic forces to switch to other crops to put food on the table. The result was that by the time prohibition was lifted in 1933, most of the bitterer cultivars best suited for cider production were lost. Beer quickly filled the resurgent demand for mildly intoxicating brews because wheat and barley take far less time to reach maturity than apple trees.

It is only now that producers in the United States are rediscovering the bitter varietals that lubricated the nation's throats from the colonial era right through until the Roaring Twenties. While many current estimates put cider at around 1% of the liquor market in the United States, with this comeback, you must ask what will happen when it reaches 2%, 3%, 5% or even 10%. While the latter percentage is unlikely any time soon, a single percent gain in market share on this scale nonetheless represents millions of additional pints consumed and perhaps a few savvy capitalists eager to invest in orchards or craft cider mills.

For hospitality, this industry 'ramp up' may present a lucrative opportunity to differentiate your beverage services from the competition. While other bars and restaurants strive to meet the modern oenophilic and cerevisaphilic demands with fancy Wineemotion™ installations and expansive craft beer lists, there's an opening for you to become a veritable 'cider center' and deliver the best in breed to this niche market. At the very least, consider testing the alcoholic waters by offering some specially imported craft or local ciders during happy hour so that customers know you are a leader in this regard.

On a side note, while the range in cider taste profiles may be less diverse than beer or wine for the time being, apples are nonetheless used throughout the culinary world (having originated from the forested flanks of Tian Shan mountains in Kyrgyzstan and Tajikistan), and new cultivars are bound to sprout. With cider as the centerpiece, you might then accent the offering with apple butter, apple marinades, apple cider vinegar-marinated meats, apple-Bourbon barbecue sauces or apple ice wine for dessert. And did we mention that apples are high in healthy fiber and vitamin C, while cider was used as a traditional remedy for colds?

Whiskeys

Yet another section not related to wine. Why are whiskeys relevant? In the same vein as micro-brewed or craft beers, they're now in vogue. Irish, Scotch, Bourbon or Rye; single malt or blended; people are on the hunt for exotic breeds and aromatic flavors. Rarity, exclusivity and experimentation give people identity and meaning in life. A cursory glance of the web will tell you that distillery locations are as diverse and globetrotting as wine appellations. If you can feed the need, this may become a powerful revenue stream for your business. Let's review some of the corollaries of investing in your whiskey selection.

Rarity: It doesn't take a lot of research to stock Johnny Walker Blue Label on the shelf – an expensive but nonetheless outstanding blended malt. As an alternative, how about offering Nikka From The Barrel, a blended whiskey from Japan? Think about this in terms of the uniqueness of the drinking experience and the element of surprise. If a whiskey brand is offered everywhere, it will not contribute to an experience that's anything out of the ordinary. Offer a rare elixir to make the occasion that much more exceptional.

Rapport: Whiskeys, like wine, require cajoling. If you expect people to throw down their doubloons on these brown liquors, you'd best keep your bartenders and waiters in the loop. Give them the knowledge to offer legitimate recommendations, which will in turn enable longer, healthier conversations to flourish, augmenting the overall guest experience.

Markup: Straightforward as it comes, whiskey by the glass can run up quite the bill. The more esoteric you get, the more opportunities you're giving customers to experience something apart from the staple (and comparatively inexpensive) brands like Wild Turkey or Canadian Club. If you've taken the time to assemble a formidable whiskey collection, people will take the time to explore that ensemble. They may get a little adventurous with their wallets, too.

Prestige: Unlike craft beers that may only be an additional talking point for guests and waitstaff, brandishing the title of 'Scotch Bar' or 'Bourbon Tavern' has an elevated, patrician aura about it. Wine will typically be a secondary consideration for patrons to your restaurant – the cuisine almost always rests at number one – unless, of course, you're renowned for housing an exhaustive cellar (no small feat we might add) or have branded yourself as an *enoteca* – Italian for 'wine shop' but quite often housing a vibrant bar or bistro section. Like wine, inspired Whiskey selections are for the true connoisseur. Such consumers will seek you out, appetizers and entrées optional. It's a niche market but it's growing.

Presentation: Heavy markups may intimidate patrons away from a purchase. Whiskeys have a long shelf though, so it's not like you have to fret over spoilage. That leaves plenty of half to three-quarters filled bottles on the shelf, and when arranged together with the right lighting, it can amount to one darn impressive display. Imagine the typical bar, stocked with the usual suspects for rum, vodka, tequila and gin. Yawn. Now add fifty bottles of whiskey, all with artistic labels and distinctive glass designs. Wow.

Pairings: Everyone loves a good pairing. Just as revamping your wine menu is a chance to also revitalize your gastronomy, the same goes for your liquors. Have fun with it. The peat-smoked zing of a fine Scotch matches exquisitely with some salty charcuterie while the dry bite of a Kentucky Bourbon pairs nicely with a tapas-style spread of cool dips and salty olives.

Again, rapport plays a part here, as educated waitstaff will always be a cardinal element towards pairings and, ultimately, customer satisfaction.

Glassware: Top-flight products deserve something better than a half-dollar tumbler or stemless wine glass. Consider martini bars. It's all about the details: an elongated bowl, a twist in the stem, an array of tinted or prechilled glasses to offset the different colors of each concoction. Transfer this thought process to whiskey. Thick-cut glass and crystal tumblers will extend your bar's aura of quality; even if it's only by a touch, these tiny touches always contribute to the greater whole we codify as ambiance.

Water: Many whiskies are consumed with a drop of water to bring the flavor out. Others like ice. Still others use *Scotch rocks*, which are frozen stones shaped like ice cubes, chilling the beverage without any dilution. Regardless of preference, this is not a tap water situation. Consider distilled water in bottled form to give assurance to patrons. This aura of quality even extends to the shape of ice cubes your machine makes – another opportunity for a unique mark.

Copy: Give your patrons something to read while they indulge themselves; it's entertainment after all. Think tasting cards with brief blurbs on every spirit's history and what flavors to expect from each sip. Yet another tiny touch to append the overall guest experience, consider integrating these factoids into the menu, but only if it doesn't amount to a cluttered read.

Constituency: Support your local producers, enough said. Although this might not bear fruit for those outside of Kentucky, Ireland or Scotland, do your research as you never know who has recently started roasting rye or wheat in your vicinity. Yes, this is a chance to develop a relationship with a new supplier and, yes, this is something to boast about. Guests the world over crave local immersion, so strive to deliver wherever possible.

Bourbon Dynasty

Even though California produces some spectacular wines and local craft beers have taken the nation by storm, no other country on the planet makes Bourbon. It is comparable to Scotch, Irish Whiskey or Canadian

Ryes in all but the primary ingredient – maize instead of malted barley or wheat – but no other country has even a remotely sophisticated sour mash culture or variety of world-class distilleries up and running. This drink is uniquely American, and like its counterparts stemming from the British Isles, Bourbon can help boost your beverage revenues.

For the record, Bourbon can be made anywhere within the United States so long as maize comprises a minimum of 51% of the raw constituents. Despite this broad stipulation, Bourbon is traditionally only made in Kentucky where it can then be labeled as Kentucky Straight Whiskey. As for the name itself, Bourbon harks back to before the Louisiana Purchase when the French were fur trapping and trading up and down the Mississippi. The Bourbon Dynasty was the ruling monarchial house of France for centuries, and while this family was all but snuffed out during the French Revolution, the title is nonetheless fitting for how popular this liquor has become.

In fact, according to DISCUS (Distilled Spirits Council of the United States), Bourbon is the fastest growing segment in the spirits market, especially among millennials and centennials. Yes, the sweet-and-sour mash bite requires a bit of an adjustment from the peaty, smoky tongue of Scotch, but the demand is there, so you might as well meet it. On the supply side, the Bourbon market is far more colorful than it was ten or even five years ago. While the staples like Jim Beam and Wild Turkey are always good to have on shelf, many previously small batch providers are now scaling up to make their bottles more readily available to a liquor supplier near you. The awareness of these lesser-known brands is also on the rise, making your job in finding tableside buyers all the easier.

We've gravitated towards New World whiskeys of late because good Scotch is becoming far too expensive for everyday consumption. No doubt many other people feel the same way, especially when a single shot at a restaurant can run you upwards of $30. Bourbon is thus a relatively inexpensive drop accompanied by a wealth of premier distillers who each add their own unique touches to the formula. With each new bottle under our belt comes exposure to a great array of rich caramel, almond or even banana aromas and equally complex notes for the tongue. Some new favorites include Eagle Rare, Old Forrester, Corner Creek, and Double Oaked Woodford Reserve. We'd be remiss if we didn't mention Pappy

Van Winkle's Family Reserve, perhaps the renowned Bourbon and bound to gather intrigue if you can source it.

Before we delve any further, though, a few questions are in order. What Bourbons have you tried? How do you think the flavors are best differentiated from other whiskeys or distilled spirits? Can you recall any cocktails, sauces or food recipes where Bourbon is a key component?

This third question is remarkable because, unlike Scotch which is chiefly enjoyed straight or with a few rocks, Bourbon is palatable both neat and as a cooking complement. Indeed, parallel to the uptick in Bourbon availability on the drink list is the appearance of a host of sour mash-infused barbecue sauces. Corn whiskeys are also making their way onto other sections of the food menu including some very appetizing desserts.

When something is trending like this, you should at the very least consider ways to hop on the bandwagon. That, or challenge your team to come up with some creative suggestions for cocktail mixology and tasty new cuisine.

The Wines of Scotland

Also known as Scotch! Seeing as how this lucrative elixir is perennially in vogue, knowing how to stock your bar appropriately can lead to greatly bolstered sales. Here are a few considerations to chew on:

Typical and Atypical: Just like how every wine list should have at least a few bottles of familiar grapes like Merlot and Chardonnay, your whiskey menu should likewise contain several commonplace brands so that neophytes aren't intimidated. Once you have this down pat, branch away from Johnny Walker and Glenfiddich by stocking some of the more niche and obscure brands to appease genuine Scotch aficionados.

Full Frontal: When done right, an array of well-lit whiskey bottles along a multi-level shelving unit will make for a very opulent display. You want your Scotch out in the open to impress all, generate curiosity and visually entice purchases.

Mixology: It's all too easy to pigeonhole Scotch as a standalone or ice-only affair. Recalling two favorites – a Manhattan and an Old

Fashioned – whiskey blending would seem to be a task for Bourbon or Rye. Now, however, creative bartenders all over the world have debunked these stereotypes, using Scotch as a main or ancillary ingredient for some rather tasty cocktails.

The Right Atmosphere: Scotch drinking is a classy affair, so make sure that everything about your ambiance is congruent to set the mood. Think wood furnishings, fireplaces, plush leather seats, felt-top divans and a suitable music playlist.

Pairings: Give people a Scotch nudge by printing whiskey pairings on the menu right beside each wine recommendation. This will subliminally compel patrons to consider Scotch as a meal lubricant or digestif rather than getting your servers to do all the heavy lifting. You might even put a Scotch tasting on the menu aligned with a party-sized sample plate of appetizers.

Scotch Tastings: Instead of relegating this to the bottom line of text on your dinner menu, why not host an event dedicated entirely to this beverage. The main objective of such an event would go far beyond a simple tasting though; it is direct advertising for your bar and your restaurant with food crafted from your in-house menu. For hotels, you could also merge this with a manager's reception, allowing guests to develop a face-to-face connection with your executive team and greatly enhance the brand connection.

Tell a Story: Not all Scotch distilleries are built along the same river valley in the highlands of Scotland. For starters, is the Scotch blended or single malt? Next consider that there are five main producing regions: Lowland, Highland, Speyside, Campbeltown and Islay – each with their own techniques, taste variations and distinct geography. Moreover, each distillery has its own vibrant history. These are all factors that contribute to the smooth, salty, smoky, peaty taste of the liquor and worth conveying to your patrons.

Small Batch Distilleries

Alcoholic beverages are far more than a vessel for inebriation. They are a pillar of the dining experience. While wine and beer are the two most common meal accompaniments in this category, there's something interesting happening in the world of spirits and other distilled elixirs. Much like that of microbreweries and limited-barrel wines, small batch distilleries are making a resurgence, and it's an opportunity you should seize.

Why? *Product differentiation.*

Your restaurant or bar may be distinguished from your competitors by its décor, its view, its ambiance, its food menu, its cocktails, its executive chef, its live music, its onsite events or a host of other features and combinations from this list, but recruiting small batch distillers is one emerging area where you can now make an impact. All the previously mentioned aspects held constant, what will differentiate your bar selection when you stock all the same standard liquors as one might find at an airport lounge a continent away – for example, Johnny Walker, Jim Beam, Bacardi, Jose Cuervo or Smirnoff.

We're not slighting these brands – they wouldn't be household names if they weren't of quality and well-marketed – but rather, because they are so prevalent around the world, they aren't doing you any favors insofar as providing your customers with a more memorable experience. It's easier to confuse two nearby pubs with the same drink slate over one which exclusively serves liquors from small batch distilleries. These spirits may not be available at the neighborhood liquor store, and they may require an adept hand in procurement.

In a lot of cases, the rarer the better, although too rare may make it near impossible to continually stock – *seasonally available* as the optimal term here. This trend has caught on with many of the more prestigious small batch distilleries already selling out their whole supply to purveyors both domestic and across the pond.

In this sense, these liquors further your restaurant or bar's reputation from its competitive set. Many of these small batch liquors may have imperceptible taste differences when compared to the table name brands, but true aficionados will be able to tell. In fact, many consumers actively seek out local or unique spirits and their resultant cocktails, giving them a reason choose your establishment over all others.

From Russia with Vodka

Vodka's main purpose in the Western World, aside from the straight-up vodka martini, is for basic mix drinks and blending – drowning out the harshness of this grain or potato distillation with loads of fructose or citric acid. Our first thoughts lean towards a vodka soda with bar lime, a Cosmo, a Screwdriver or a Bloody Mary. And occasionally, when celebrations are in order, the twentysomethings among us might take it as a shot.

Contrary to popular belief, there is a substantial variety in vodkas, and upscale brands are meant for sipping. Many of these finer bottles seldom reach crates for export. Fortunately, there are also outstanding vodkas from many countries like Sweden, France, Poland and North America. (For the foreseeable future as we write this amidst the ongoing conflict in Ukraine, buying from Russia, the largest producer of this clear liquor, is simply not in the cards.)

It's time we changed vodka's perception, or at the very least enlighten our guests as to the cultural traditions of our friends in Eastern Europe. In those parts of the world – where its consumption oftentimes outpaces beer, wine and other spirits combined at over three gallons per person per annum – vodka is consumed neat, either by the mouthful or, when it is made by true craftsmen, its bite is soft enough so that it can be casually imbibed drop after drop alongside a meal. Sipping a high-end vodka with caviar is a luxurious experience everyone should enjoy at least once in their lives. They've even coined the term 'vodka belt' to describe the region where this is common practice, including pretty much all of Eastern Europe as well as the Baltic and Nordic states.

Think for a moment about your bar's selection of whiskeys. It's normal for people to order a glass of this spirit on the rocks or neat. Why can't vodka be the same? It's a no-brainer to assume that putting one or two high-end vodkas on the menu might better appease customers by giving them an option.

The biggest step to initiate a vodka-centric paradigm shift is in the sourcing. The most commercial and international brands of this liquor are not necessarily the most flavorful. They are engineered for scale and mixing. This is not what you want. You want a vodka that stands on its own.

Start by looking for a brand off the beaten path. I'd also suggest that you find one with an alcohol percentage around 40% but not directly on the mark. This way, people won't be intimidated by a spirit with too high an ABV while its unusual proof (that is, not precisely 40% or 80 proof) will heighten its allure. Specifically for certain establishments, know that vodka pairs excellently with oysters and other components of a seafood tower; train your staff accordingly so that they know what aperitif to recommend for these appetizers.

Alcohol Alternatives

As restaurateurs and hoteliers, you have a serious obligation to ensure that your guests do not drink and drive, especially if hard liquor has been ordered to a table. Legal penalties are significant. The good news is that there are zero-alcohol alternatives, and these alternatives are growing in both availability and quality.

Concurrently, the number of people abstaining from alcohol – either fully or curtailing their frequency per week – is growing. Whether for health reasons or otherwise, such patrons may look favorably upon anything beyond sodas or carbonated water – like mocktails or freshly squeezed juice concoctions – as to way to augment their meal experiences. With the growth of wellness, wellbeing and nutrition during the pandemic, this trend is bound to only increase over the decade ahead.

Domestically in the United States, the alcoholic beverage market is approximately one quarter trillion dollars (2021 data). Growing quickly, the alcohol alternative beverage market or imitation beverages like zero-alcohol wine, beer and spirits is estimated at $29 billion, roughly one tenth the size. To put this in perspective, the alcoholic alternative market is equal to the sum of all 'brown' spirits – Bourbon, Irish Whisky, Scotch, Brandy, Cognac, Canadian Rye and others (data sources: Statistica and DISCUS).

For those familiar with the television series *The Simpsons*, the secret rooftop garden was accessible through the fake door on the Kwik-E-Mart's non-alcoholic beer cooler because no one really drank those products, at least according to Homer Simpson. Oh, how times have changed since that episode (titled "Lisa the Vegetarian" for those with a Disney+ subscription) aired in late 1995.

Nowadays, spirit alternatives such as Seedlip, a gin equivalent with an expanding lineup of plant-based liquor substitutes, have made a tremendous impact in the marketplace. According to Seedlip's website, their first product is based on the distilled non-alcoholic remedies from "The Art of Distillation" written in 1651 by John French.

As another example, Jukes Cordialities produces several of what we may call wine equivalents. They happen to be organic apple cider vinegar-based drinks made through the maceration of vegetables, fruits, herbs, spices and flowers and with no fermentation. Wine professional Matthew Jukes created these drinks because he felt that dealcoholized wines fell so far short of the mark he had to come up with a totally different style of drink to please sophisticated palates. The result is a suite of drinks that have complex fruit and spice notes, akin to some of those flavors found in wine, coupled with genuine richness on the palate and also a dry aftertaste.

The opportunity for your mixologist is to develop non-alcoholic cocktails based on these and others, recognizing the potential for additional revenues per cover as well as satisfaction enhancement. Much like how the growth of veganism and vegetarianism influence a group's selection of restaurants, so too will the presence of alcohol alternatives for the non-drinkers in a party. Moreover, by promoting these risk-free products within your cocktail list, your designated driver will no longer be relegated to soft drinks (often served at zero cost to said driver).

These are all good reasons to investigate your options. And you can go one step further by making the project a teambuilding exercise, transforming it into a contest for your bar staff to determine the final selection of non-alcoholic drinks.

WINE AND CUISINE

Cheese Tastings

Cheese is often thought of as the lowly second-tier cousin to the eponymous grape-based libation, even though the two go hand-in-hand across the globe for fancy soirees of the wine and cheese variety. Take a closer look and you'll see that the craft and sophistication behind these semisolid dairy products goes just as deep as their alcoholic pairings. Swiss, Ricotta, Gorgonzola, Parmigiano, Pecorino, Bocconcini, Asiago, Gouda, Stilton, Gruyère, Camembert, Mozzarella, Havarti, Halloumi, Feta, you name it.

Our appreciation for the depth of cheese in this manner was sparked many summers ago when we sojourned to Cannes, France. While shacked up at a bucolic Relais & Châteaux property, Hotel Le Mas Candille, in the town of Mougins, we needed only to walk downstairs ten paces to reach the entrance of a Michelin Star-rated restaurant, Le Candille, headed at the time by celebrated chef Serge Gouloumès.

Most notable at first glance was the prefixed menu at over 400 Euro per head. Not only are we talking about a truly empyrean bill (considering that this trip occurred before the recent recession, inflation scare and subsequent European currency reevaluation), but wine pairings were not included and tallied at an additional 200 Euro per head.

Jaw-droppingly expensive? Yes. A meal that we'll never forget? Also, yes. This was not a restaurant but a gastronomic adventure that took four hours from start to finish. We never thought pigeon could be this tasty. For dessert, we all enjoyed a marshmallow tasting as a precursor to our edible gold foil-wrapped sugar cane birdcages encasing marzipan canaries.

Aside from the utterly exquisite appetizers, mains and sweets, one striking feature was the cheese tray. Supplementary to the uncorking of our first glass of wine, a knowledgeable server wheeled over a cart adorned with sixty different types of Brie. That's right, all these delectable slices of dairy heaven representing only one distinct type of cheese from different producers, all joined by a few select honeys, jams, jellies and home-baked crackers.

Two caveats. First, this is France, home to a millennia-old tradition of proud cheesemaking with each town's produce as unique as the next. Second, we were at a Two Star Michelin-rated restaurant and we doubt the cheese cart would make a similar appearance at the nearest McDonald's, to say the least. These two aside, what really struck us was the breadth of knowledge that the server effused after a couple of generic prompts. In fact, he was no simple waiter, but an in-house *affineur de fromage* – an individual specifically responsible for the maturation and aging of cheeses. Think of him like a sommelier but for cheese.

Reminiscing on this experience years later, we have now attended several recent wine tastings where each varietal was appropriately paired with a different cheese to complement and enhance the flavors of both. It's a trendy approach to flights, with wine vendors rapidly linking up with cheesemongers, adding catchy descriptors like artisanal, boutique, craft and farmstead to increase the allure and price.

For your own outlet, consider a *horizontal tasting* – one where guests cross-compare cheeses of the same type and region but made from different producers. Alternatively, a *vertical tasting* is one where you sample the cheeses (or wines for that matter) from the same producer across a spectrum of different ages.

While at Le Candille, we completed a vertical Brie tasting, each cheese wild with classic creamy flavor and pungent differences in saltiness and sourness. Not only will we never forget this experience, but it has also forever heightened our intrinsic level of cheese appreciation. In psychological terms, this is what you would call a *transformative experience* – one that leaves the participant better off and more self-actualized upon its completion.

Knowing that premium cheeses are officially a burgeoning commodity, are your patrons ready? Would a cheese tasting on the menu sell? Would specially selected cheeses augment the perceived value of a wine flight? At the ultra-luxury end of things, would your restaurant benefit from staffing an affineur de fromage alongside your somm? Perhaps, just as you offer wine by the glass, you can likewise recommend 'cheese by the slice' as an accompaniment.

Wine and Tomato Tastings

Why would any restaurant engage in an experiential program like a tasting? These not only drive revenues but help give a dining outlet 'legs'. Everyone who lives in an urban area can attest to the comings and goings of the restaurant world. It's a tough industry and you need surefire reasons for customers to return time and again when they have so many other choices at their disposal.

For instance, a new Italian eatery opens to much aplomb. It gets rave reviews while you, the customer, struggle to get a reservation within the first few months of its launch. Then when you finally try it, it meets or surpasses your expectations, but never gives you a concrete reason to return anytime soon or to go out of your way to recommend it to your friends.

In the typical cycle of a half a decade, this Italian restaurant's limelight fades until it's only marginally profitable, with only a few places achieving continued, ironclad popularity in the face of a perpetual renewal of the area's competition. Everyone likes the shiny new toy, after all. While this process can benefit the average patron who is afforded a constant refresh of neighborhood dining options, it's a headache for anyone in the business.

Regardless of the industry, launching a new product is a nightmare, and not for those who value their sleep. Moreover, the influx of successive batches of ever-inventive restaurant concepts is only truly sustainable in boom times. When the market goes bust, however, many outlets find themselves fighting over scraps as customers opt for home cooking over spending their money eating out or ordering in.

In times of economic hardship, your restaurant needs that x-factor to keep the turns coming. Tastings represent but one solid prospect in this regard because they add an educational and transformative component beyond merely exciting and delighting the taste buds. They can give your eatery that wow moment to help make it evergreen and recession-proof. Importantly for this goal, specific food tastings help to promote beverage pairings to thereby increase the average guest cheque.

It should thus come as no surprise why cheese tastings, charcuterie boards, wine flights and beer flights are such hot items on the menu these days. And of course, you can get as esoteric or regionally specific as you so desire — for example, arriving in Stockholm on summer vacation and enjoying a lovely five-part Nordic herring tasting.

To highlight one other au courant example, the concept of a tomato tasting is one of those strange attractors because it pertains to an agricultural produce with near-universal appeal and culinary usage, and yet one that has never commanded the same veneration as, say, grapes for wine or milk for cheese. It's about time the lowly tomato gets the respect it deserves.

Moreover, with a strong diversity of cultivars that can be grown practically wherever the sun shines as well as the movement towards heirloom varieties that command greater appreciation through their diversity of shapes and colors, setting up a tomato tasting as an appetizer option may not seem as outlandish as you initially think. Add to your tomato board – or any such tasting – some artisanal breads, sweet sauces and fresh herbs, and the taste buds will be all but crying for a wash of alcohol.

Our advice is to get creative about what types of differential tastings you can provide for your guests that combine great wine with the best of your kitchen. Talk to your local suppliers to see what they can source. If you've never run a program like this at your restaurant, start with something more perfunctory like a cheeseboard to serve as a moneymaker and as part of the learning process.

Tomatoes and Cheese

Many hotel properties and rural restaurants nowadays also have their own gardens to adequately satisfy the farm-to-table trend. If you are up to it, we would highly recommend you dig a few holes for tomatoes. They're delicious, have a wide variety of different cultivars and, like cheese, olives and bread, pair exquisitely with wine.

We were inspired to discuss this coupling after many recent nights out at Italian restaurants where a big platter of tomatoes with fresh and aged cheeses were handed out as appetizer. A Caprese salad is, after all, many people's favorite. Such communal plates instantly energize a table, heightening the dining experience and hastening alcohol consumption.

Together, tomatoes and cheese represent a traditional-yet-simple and colorful complement to a glass of wine. They also give you a chance to show off your local pride. Even though cheese is considered the premier food companion to wine, tomatoes are likewise excellent because of their versatility.

Consumed raw, you have the classic reds coming in many different shapes, shades, and sizes, but you also have the heirlooms in pink, orange, green (also consider tomatillos), pale yellow, gold (hence the Italian name for tomato, pomodoro, which roughly translates as 'apple of gold') and even purple-indigo varietals. Add to those cooked versions such as oven-roasted, grilled, smoked, fried and sundried. Then you have the sauces and tapenades which go far beyond simple red marinara with numerous European sauces in addition to all the different New World salsas.

We eat with our eyes as much as we do our mouths (and nostrils), so tapping into the full tomato spectrum will make for an especially pleasing treat and fodder for social media amplification. Plus, variety adds some fun to the plate insofar as mixing and matching. Giving people the chance to try different combinations of cheeses, tomatoes, tomato sauces, jams, honeys, olives, artisanal bread slices, crackers and so on adds an extra layer of interactivity and sociability to the dining experience. In essence, you are giving people the ingredients and it's up to them to discover what fits their palates best. Wash it all down with a hearty bottle of white or red wine, of course.

And this is the broad lesson when it comes to food and wine pairings of any sort. They should be designed to be complementary, meaning that the grouping should be greater than the sum of its parts. Wine is hardly just a sophisticated source of ethanol intoxication. By diligently pairing a particular drop with the specific flavors, you amplify the whole meal. And guests are relying on your servers and sommeliers to steer them appropriately.

Beer and Cheese

Nowadays, with the resurgence of microbreweries and local beers, beer has really come into its own as an alcoholic beverage with as much diversity as its grape-born cousin. Another emerging trend (at least from a North American perspective) is to substitute wines for beers in cheese tastings. It's not just tastings for you to consider, but ways to pair piquant beers with savory mains or cheese boards as meal accompaniments.

All told, there are plenty of opportunities to mix and match beers and cheeses for a potential upsell. Moreover, some people are staunch beer drinkers and won't ever be swiftly coerced over to the wine camp. Don't fight them; oblige them. Give people the same diversity of options for beers as you would wine. The rule of thumb for pairing beers with cheeses is *like begets like.* This is what most cicerones will tell you, but there's far too much leniency for this statement to be considered gospel.

Mild cheeses including creamy varieties like anything goat, Queso Oaxaca, Mozzarella or Camembert will work swimmingly with smooth, high acidity brews like wheat beers, pale lagers, fruit beers or even ciders. Also consider how you combine textures – buttery, soft cheeses might contrast too sharply with a heavily carbonated beer. There's latitude here, however. The nutty, fruity undertones of a light cheese also mix well with the sweet caramel flavors of light-bodied, roasted brown ale.

When it comes to pairings, brown ales should probably be called grays because the matching rules are incredibly loose. Yes, browns work with gooey cheeses, but they also work with dry, hard, leathery or tangy cheeses like Cheddar, Gruyère, Gouda or any other slice with concentrated flavor. But the more intense you get with your cheeses, so too must you consider earthy, weighty brews with more malt and hops like Stouts and Porters as well as bitter, drier drafts like Pilsners. Further, a little carbonation can go miles here to cleanse the palate before the next bite.

At the far end of the spectrum, stinky blue or washed-rind cheeses should, in most cases, be married with a very strong beer – IPAs or Trappist Ales. Depending on the strength of its bite, a floral IPA can also mesh with a sharp Provolone or salty, aged Cheddar. You might also consider pairing according to region – Stilton with a bottle of London Pride or a wedge of Chimay with a pint of Orval, both from Belgium.

Again, there's a lot of flexibility. And part of the point is to have fun with it, because if you are having fun then that enthusiasm will be transferred to your patrons. All in the name of offering a better overall dining experience which will ultimately mean more sales.

Olives and Other Accompaniments

There's a short expression in Italian we're fond of – *l'ambiente del vino*. The direct translation is 'the ambiance of wine' but really it means so much more. We are, after all, emotional beings and no experience occurs in a vacuum. As such, the taste and enjoyment of a particular glass of wine is not only influenced by the blend of various grape varietals and the liquid's color or smell but also the glass it's served in, the bottle it's poured from, the table setting, the company you keep, the setting in which it's enjoyed and, of course, the food it's paired with.

While every restauranteur understands (or should!) the basic principle of food and wine pairings, we've seldom seen anyone aside from executive chefs, sommeliers and F&B directors wholly embrace the potential for one to augment the other and help to drive meal satisfaction as well as incremental purchases. Maybe that's why these individuals reach the top of the ladder, but nevertheless it's your duty to pay that knowledge and passion forward to the entire team so that they can convey this principle to your patrons.

We'll leave the actual meal pairings to your diligent culinary team as this require a much more substantial conversation. For now, let's focus on snacks – or in more sophisticated terms, *meal accompaniments* – and how they might influence a guest's overall satisfaction with their beverage selection as well as perhaps entice them to try something that's a tad pricier.

We specifically reference olives because, aside from cheese, they are the most traditional nosh to accompany an aperitif or BTG order and because Western countries are on the cusp of understanding, much like wine, how diverse olives truly are. If you think in terms of the ambiance with which you present your liquor selection, would you present any old bowl of olives, or would you offer your customers a platter with their choice of three different cultivars such as Kalamata, Niçoise or Manzanilla? Simply including the named modifier or place of origin in the description (either on the menu or communicated verbally) might be enough to convince many patrons of the food's greater quality, thus substantiating a higher price point.

Similarly, the same applies to nearly any other snack you might serve. Ask any chef or foodie. An olive is never just an olive; a tomato is never just a tomato; a cracker is never just a cracker. Over the past few years, we've noted the proliferation of elaborate classifications on menus for cured meats, vegetables, fruits, nuts, legumes, honeys, sauces and just about any other edible item you can put in your mouth. Specificity is storytelling, and stories are what sell. Why not try putting an 'olive board' on the menu as an appetizer in lieu of the more expected cheeseboard?

Chocolate and Wine Pairings

We all know that chocolate is a highly romantic food; it's an aphrodisiac primarily due to its high concentrations of theobromine, a caffeine relative as well as a serotonin and dopamine activator. Why not bring chocolate and wine together?

While you may not have any many options as, say, a wine and cheese tasting, pairing chocolate with any grape-based liquor can help you win the hearts and minds of incoming guests. You can apply this concept for an amuse bouche, appetizer, dessert or as part of the main if a key ingredient is a bitterer expression of the cacao bean.

Furthermore, much like any other edible staple with a bourgeois cachet, chocolate is also going through an artisanal revolution. There's now a plethora of high percentage dark, organic and single-origin labels, with culinary specialists all over the world concocting playful and delicious blends of quality chocolate and some very esoteric flavor concoctions.

Not only can you offer a range of chocolates organized by purity (say, 90% or 65%) or country of origin (for example, Colombia versus Ivory Coast), but also some outright wild horizontal tastings from the same chocolatier. As a start, include common additives like caramel, dried fruit, nougat, ganache, mint, cinnamon, nuts (beware of allergies!), berries, peanut butter or liqueur. Then, look beyond to real standout ingredients like tropical fruit, ginger, maple syrup, bacon, wasabi, popcorn, pretzel bits, tea leaves or flower petals. With all these options, you may only need to consider a chocolate-only tasting and leave the digestif to the guest's discretion.

To contrast this with the perfunctory cheese pairings, you must take note that dark chocolate has a strong, sweet and bitter taste with none of the creamy or grassy notes that dairy provides. As such, there's far less flexibility when it comes to suitable wine accompaniments. You need a pungent drop to make a copacetic match. Even though we live by the motto that any wine is better than no wine, we still wouldn't recommend Pinot Noir, Sauvignon Blanc any other soft, dry varietal for this job.

To give you an example of how this might work, look to Lindt's *Paintings with Excellence* in collaboration with the popular Californian winemaker J. Lohr. While softer bottles like Pinot Noir and Merlot are still on the menu, they are appropriately countered with tangy confectionaries, while their fruitier chocolate products are paired off with fragrant, sugary white wines – namely, Chardonnay and Riesling.

Things get complicated when you consider white chocolate, milk chocolate, truffles and desserts lacking any cocoa ingredients but should nonetheless be included in any move for a wine-themed upsell (think crème brûlée, panna cotta, traditional tiramisu or cheesecake). Our final piece of advice, though, is this is that you can never go wrong with good chocolate.

The Problem with Food Wines

It happens all too often now. We're dining with friends or business associates, and we are all in need of a libation – not a full bottle but merely opting to go BTG. To help you visualize a particular instance, let's say we choose a glass of Pinot Noir.

We give it a swirl then a deep sniff and finally a good slosh to determine if it's to our liking. Sadly, a lot of restaurant wines barely pass the test. But then again, most wines are designed for everyday drinkers, with the amount of labor required to make a symphony-in-your-mouth beverage very often justifying a price point unattainable by almost all diners on a regular basis.

"Well, it's a Pinot. Nothing great but it'll do," one of us says to the server, who politely nods in agreement while already slinking away to end the conversation, "Yeah, but it's a good food wine."

And there it is. A two-word buzz phrase that is now the de rigueur excuse for allowing any piece of plonk onto the wine list – marketing puffery at its finest. Think about it for a moment; name one wine that doesn't pair well with food? In fact, an argument could be made that wine was first invented then regionally perfected to work in harmony with a given area's produce. In essence, when someone says that a certain label is a *food wine*, deep down what they are really saying is that it's garbage because you need to shove some snacks down your throat just to wash out its asphyxiating aftertaste.

And don't get us started on food wines being good palate cleansers. Any beverage from carbonated water to hallucinogenic absinthe can be categorized as that. The fact remains that a vintage should stand on its own and shouldn't have to rely on any solid complements for its enjoyment.

Luckily, the average customer hasn't yet caught on to the gilded blunder of this terminology. But just like how we now sneer at receiving jug wine or table wine when dining out, this phrase will quickly start to garner the proper amount of scorn it deserves. Ergo, you had best make your sommelier and your servers aware that 'food wine' will soon be *verbum non gratum* (Latin for 'a word not welcome').

Our diatribe aside, the underlying point is that, for your menu to truly shine, all your beverages must be able to hold their own. True, there are places where volume is the game of the name, but in most cases, we are all trying to deliver an elevated product that the entire team is proud to stand behind while every customer goes home feeling fulfilled. To this end, you simply must take meticulous care in curating the best possible wine list. If it isn't working, let your inventory of that bottle run out and don't restock, lest you are left with a bunch of forgettable food wines that won't serve your brand.

Choosing a Restaurant from the Wine

The normal thought pattern when choosing a restaurant is to think about the location, price point, ambiance and type of cuisine, with a great wine selection as a value-add but not a primary determinant. What if wine was a key factor?

For the foreseeable future, it's unlikely that most patrons will start to search for dining options based upon the availability of specific vintages. But they may be on the lookout for a place that combines great food and great wine. By putting wine front and center as a tool for deploying zero-cost marketing and building a cachet to become a price leader, you can get to a point where people are mentioning your restaurant in passing with something akin to, "This place has incredible wine, so let's go there."

A heuristic like this takes a fully committed wine program and an equally adept marketing team to pull off. Still, it's a powerful statement that will differentiate your product beyond the talents of your executive chef, the attentiveness of your servers and the six-figure-plus renovation you completed during the pandemic shutdown to invigorate the space.

Besides getting a mention in a local food blog that lists off the top ten wine-focused restaurants, one of the beauties about being known for having an impressive cellar or by-the-glass selection – as opposed to, for instance, being known for tasty tacos – is that it attracts high-margin wine drinkers. And this subset of diners isn't stopping in for just a black coffee and a single pastry.

Besides a thorough review of your menu and marketing pizzazz, we offer one other consideration that we've seen yield succeed – arranging the menu by wine flavor profiles instead of by the customary starters, mains and desserts format. For this, imagine having the food menu organized under subheadings which read as, 'Sweet and Fruity', 'Buttery White', 'Light-Bodied Red' and 'Bold, Dark and Full'.

It's a radical approach that's sure to leave an impression, and that's the point. The pandemic has eroded regular buying habits and customer loyalty. Google and online ordering apps have made it as easy as a few extra taps to try out another restaurant, versus sticking to your local dining spot, along with all the psychological safety from knowing what you're getting.

During a post-pandemic reopening or revitalization, with every restaurant clamoring to fill tables, you must stand apart from the pack. While this menu reshuffling idea may not be exactly to your liking, it should get you thinking about what's actually feasible for your specific situation. The broader objective for a wine-first menu would not only be to sell more wine by nudging beverage sales in that direction, but to further distinguish your property's restaurant as an institution committed to offering only the best to its patrons. Specific cellar recommendations and educational snippets inserted into the menu also reinforces this mission.

WINE PRESENTATION

By the Glass Strategy

One of the luxuries of self-isolation during the pandemic was that it afforded us all the chance to drink down our cellars. The two of us also took the time to genuinely converse with a few friends who happened to be wine merchants with a few extra bottles on hand to put together some taster packs. Upon sampling these individual bottles, it made us think about how wine purchasing behaviors have changed in the post-pandemic.

While discussing what would compel the average person to start buying by the case versus only by the individual bottle is a topic unto itself, our fear is that in a period of sharp economic decline and uncertainty, many restaurants will struggle to convert BTG patrons into purchasing a full bottle. Sometimes you just won't succeed on this front.

Thus, it would be prudent for all dining outlets to have a solid BTG strategy so that revenues and customer satisfaction are never compromised. Thinking not only as an adaptation to the long tail of the coronavirus, but also that people in general are drinking less alcohol, so you need sound tactics to get them from one glass to two and from two to more.

It goes without saying that all guests should drink responsibly and not get behind the wheel after they are approaching the legal alcohol consumption limit. At the same time, though, most restaurant operations require alcoholic beverage revenues to keep the business afloat. As food and associated costs are often breakeven, getting people to drink more is not a topic we can shy away from. Prudence and waitstaff training are essential.

In fact, this is one of the more fun aspects of working as hotel asset managers because it has let us work alongside many brilliant sommeliers and restaurant managers to come back with a BTG program that delights patrons and delivers on the income statement. Here are what make for a great BTG program:

Short: Keep the options for red and white highly limited. The more you put on the BTG menu, the harder it will be to manage inventory and the longer patrons will take in making their orders. You want the decision to be a no-brainer while at the same time not putting too much of a burden on the server to remember the key selling details for each bottle.

Simple: While brevity can allude to simplicity, there are other aspects that contribute to the latter definition, including legibility in font as well as estate name and region identification. Namely, people are less likely to order when they are confused, or they will take up more of the server's time to possibly impede service at other tables.

Diverse: Even though it motivates sales when names of bottles are readily understood, this does not mean you should resort to only those wine varietals or brands that are internationally known. You need a bit of flair for the more adventurous drinkers. Be bold, offering a reasonable BTG variety, then your wine list will become renowned in its own right.

Anchored: Some people will only ever buy the cheapest item on the menu and that's not a habit you can change. However, you can deploy the principles of *anchor pricing* to your BTG program by juxtaposing a more lavish offering against a less-expensive option to make the latter look like a better deal to your spendthrift customers.

Extra: It's not uncommon for restaurants to use the BTG menu to help get rid of remnant stock. While this is a wholly salubrious tactic to take, the one caution is that you first have a solid updating process in place, both for inventory and website management. If you don't, it will look highly unprofessional for your online wine listings to be out of sync with the paper menu or, worse, for the paper menu to be wrong. If you are cycling through unwanted inventory on a weekly or biweekly basis, make the BTG page an insert that can be updated at any time by the restaurant manager or sommelier, and leave your BTG selections off your website. QR codes also work quite well here, although they don't fit with high-end branding.

Choose Your Wine Glass Wisely

"You have chosen...wisely," is what the immortal knight says to Indiana Jones after he drinks from the Holy Grail – an unsuspecting wooden cup hidden among a swath of poisonous chalices and jeweled goblets.

We're reminded of this scene at the climax of *The Last Crusade* whenever we make a decision as to how best to pair a chosen wine with suitable glassware. Not that it is a blatant faux pas to mismatch wine and glass (at least not in our circle of friends), but proper etiquette should be followed wherever possible. Not only do shape and size affect aroma and flavor via a series of complex molecular interactions, but they offer a strong visual demarcation to augment the overall drinking experience.

Just Google any listing of wine glass styles and it's apparent that there are quite a few more types of glasses than you might have stocked at your restaurant. You might only carry white and red glasses (and flutes for Champagne), in which case it would serve you well to source perhaps one or two more types so that differential wine orders are given a visually different treatment.

Think of it as the wine's garnish. Imagine a couple dining out, one orders a Zinfandel while the other gets a Cabernet Sauvignon. If you present both in the same glassware, there will be little insofar as visible demarcation as both varietals' purple-red colorations are practically indistinguishable to the layperson or harried server. Now pour the Zinfandel in standard red and the Cabernet Sauvignon in a oblong Bordeaux wine glass – a drastically augmented and more complex drinking experience for both patrons. These effects would be even more pronounced for, say, a guest with a Gewürztraminer, presented in a traditional Alsace glass, sitting opposite someone with white wine in a wide Chardonnay glass.

From the sheer variety of choices, it's also easy to go overboard to the point where you are confusing your servers. Expand as you see fit; the main takeaway is that when it comes to wine, beer, cocktails, coffee, tea or even milkshakes, we drink with our eyes as much as we do our mouths. Presentation matters: it influences perceived value as well as what you can charge.

Lastly, there has been a recent change towards the more casual tumbler-style of stemless glasses. These are appropriate as a bistro-style affair, and you might want to consider them for after hours or for other informal settings like alfresco dining. But they should not be utilized for fine dining or with expensive wine; in these cases, it may come off as insulting.

Show Me the Bottle!

Research has shown that if someone likes the way a bottle looks, they will also be more prone to liking the way it tastes. It's all a matter of personal identification. You may recall the fabled lesson, 'Don't judge a book by its cover', and so we can adapt this to likewise say, 'Don't judge a bottle by its label'.

Alas, we may be giving the buyer too much credit. The average consumer is apparently unable to uncouple looks from flavor. Knowing these two senses are irrevocably linked, though, a slight modification of your service standards can be applied to enhance meal satisfaction and increase sales.

First, let's talk wine by the glass. You have your brief list of available reds and whites; your servers have completed basic training to discuss key features, tasting notes and narrative details of each. But when patrons choose one wine or another, instead of proceeding straight to the question of how big a pour these customers want, now we can insert an extra step, knowing full well that it is integral to meal satisfaction.

Show them the bottle. And don't just flash it before stowing it back on the shelf. Be patient and take the time to display the artistic creativity of the label. Place it on the bar countertop or the table and let the guest touch it for a proper inspection. It's a few extra moments spent on your part but heightening the design-flavor connection may end up being the wildcard that will convince a patron to order another round.

Now consider the applications here for full bottle orders. The traditional procedure is to craft the wine list, have the sommelier or server make recommendations on said list to customers, present the selected bottle, open said bottle right away and have one person do a perfunctory tasting before pouring for the rest of the table.

But what if upon seeing the chosen bottle, the customer didn't like the label? Suppose a customer orders an expensive Old World wine, but when the bottle appears, it doesn't have the classic design of heavily scripted fonts on an off-white background with minimal iconography or stenciling. Such a mental disconnect between geography and print composition can induce confusion and anxiety. What then?

This creeping sense of *buyer's remorse* may silently hinder maximal enjoyment of the wine, thereby stymying further purchases. And if the wine is perceived as mediocre, then this could halo onto the food and ultimately onto whether a patron recommends your restaurant. It's a slippery slope.

Armed with this new insight, however, you would be wise to do your best to avoid any psychological follies. As a start, upon physical presentation, you could have your servers ask, "What do you think of the label?" Again, be patient, handing over the unopened bottle and letting the guest feel it in their hands. In this way, inquiring about the design itself will help to elucidate any consternations before popping the top, so that the waiter can then be ready to go back and select another bottle with a different design.

Then there are other tech-centric solutions such as transposing your entire wine list onto a tablet app whereby guests can not only browse through names, varietals and vintages but also bottle designs, subliminally prescreening any that they may not agree with and thus potentially cripple meal satisfaction. There are other benefits to such apps including better inventory management and analytics, so this is a project worth consideration.

There's a bigger conversation to be had here in terms of ensuring that the style of label designs for all wines matches the personality and theme of your restaurant, but this is a far more intensive goal and often one so far down the list that it's barely important. For now, though, tableside bottle presentation will always come down to staff training.

Don't Judge a Wine by Its Bottle

Again, we apply the riff on the classical adage, 'Don't judge a book by its cover,' but this time let's examine this more common expression a bit closer to see how it applies to wine, spirits and the pursuit of restaurant profits.

We are told not to base our opinions or conclusions about objects and individuals solely on their outward appearance because there is often far more happening beneath the surface worthy of our consideration if you were only to give said object or person a chance. It's a valuable piece of advice, hence why it sticks.

But its popularity, aside from its terse and catchy qualities, can be attributed to the fact that we humans are hardwired to make snap judgments based entirely on superficial qualities. The phrase has near-universal applicability because we are genetically programmed to make shortcuts in our decision-making mental processes – a trait that is highly beneficial when, say, debating whether to run from a pack of snarling wolves, but less so in a civilized setting where higher thought is required.

Regrettably, our Cro-Magnon brains can only evolve so quickly, and as such we are left with many objectionable side effects. At first brush, you will deem a man in a suit to be more successful than one in baggy gym clothes with slouched posture. A car that looks sleek will be considered faster than a boxier counterpart. A book with an artfully designed cover will sell more at its launch than one with a mediocre cover. And most people can't help but favor wines with colorful labels, fun fonts or slightly irregular bottle shapes.

Humans are slaves to our own superficiality and any resultant attribution biases that emerge. This may seem misanthropic but it's actually a good thing for our species. If we weren't making snap judgments all the time, we'd be stuck deliberating on ideas and actions to the point where we wouldn't get anything done.

Backtracking a little, we say 'most' people because even though most of us would like to view ourselves as having a sophisticated knowledge of wine and a developed food palate to boot, the sad fact is that most of us are still living in the dark ages when it comes to oenophilia. Unless they have a reference guide on hand or a sommelier certification at home in a picture frame, 99% of patrons you encounter won't be able to tell good from great wine, nor would they have any success in a blind tasting. (Larry tested his palate at an Opimian Society – a Canadian wine club with over 15,000 members – blind tasting many years ago where he placed third, a proud result.)

Customers will come to your restaurant with only a vague notion of what they already like and a budget to work within. Their judgment about what bottle to get, or to even buy a drink in the first place, will be based mostly on sticker shock, menu design, bottle design, each wine or spirit's actual name, their moods at the time and any rapport with your staff. Only some of these attributes are within your control, and for each we can then discern how to best leverage or overcome a particular social fallacy.

To start, sticker shock pertains to the relationship between your customer's wallet or outlook on spending and the dollar value listed on the menu. Although you have tangential control over how spendthrift your average patron is via the brand positioning of the restaurant, there is only so much you can do to help someone avoid sticker shock as inventory price controls are expertly honed by a purchasing manager or F&B director to be as fair as possible.

Naming has similar limits whereby a certain guest will have a preexisting affinity for a specific country of origin or the nomenclature of a certain winery and its oeuvre. But even then, you can manipulate your offerings to fit customer expectations. You may decide, for instance, that because you operate a hip, urban joint, every bottle in stock should have an equally funky name to enhance the branding. Changing your entire inventory in this manner is not advisable, though, because it's a hefty expenditure for marginal returns. Instead, knowing that some people will purchase by name alone means that you should have a 'diverse cast' on the menu.

With bottles kept in the cellar and out of sight for most restaurants, purchases are made based upon the way wines are presented on the menu, their list prices and the waiter's recommendations. When the bottle arrives at the table, the expectation is a standardized Bordeaux or Burgundy shape with a classic mix of serif and script fonts on a white-background label. Any deviations from this will be met with surprise and likely augment the dining experience by offering a bit of extra visual stimulation. While we would never advocate filling the cantina with only the most bizarre designs around, much like with naming, a few oddball additions purposefully approved for their eccentric shapes, bottle colors and sticker artwork can certainly prove to be beneficial.

Most within your control and what's cheapest to remedy are your menus and what your servers bring to the table. For the former, there are lots of psychological tricks you can use to further imbue your branding, downplay the price of a spirit or even coerce guests to select certain bottles over others. Give your art directors an idea of what you hope to accomplish then let them work their magic.

Next, suppose, for example, that a group has narrowed down its wine selection to two choices. A smart waiter might then bring over both bottles for a little show and tell. Armed with the above facts about our inherent superficiality, this staff member would likely be more conscious of any prejudgments based on bottle design alone, and then allay these thoughts by addressing them outright or through a series of moving statements.

Any which way you put it, snap decision making based on surface appearances will permeate every aspect of your revenues, not just your wine and liquor sales. Hopefully, by accepting that we are all subject to these cognitive limitations, we can then push past them for healthier returns on your restaurant covers.

Buying Wine at Auction

The wine auction market affords you an opportunity to add bottles to the restaurant's cellar that may not be available through conventional means, namely continual repurchasing orders through wine merchants. A restaurant can use auctions to fill in vintage years missing from a particular château or adding some 'spice' to a wine list with interesting, cult or hard-to-find bottles. Thanks to the internet, you can participate in auctions all over the globe. Just be mindful of shipping costs and import taxes or duties.

To guide you some guidance, we sought out an expert in this area, Stephen Ranger, who has ownership positions in two leading Canadian auction houses. Stephen is considered the country's most prominent fine wine auctioneer, lending his expertise to numerous charitable and cultural organizations each year.

Is an auction a good place for a hotel restaurant to purchase wine?
For restaurants that want to build world-class wine lists without having to hold inventories for literally years or decades, the auction market has become increasingly attractive. While the dictum of caveat emptor, or buyer beware, still holds true, auction houses base their reputation on the quality of products delivered to their clients. The best auction houses engage in extensive due diligence to ensure wines brought to auction are of impeccable provenance and have been stored in suitable conditions to ensure optimum aging and condition. Buying at auction requires a proactive engagement with the market that many smaller owners may not have time for. Many auction houses engage in-house concierges to assist both trade and private clients make good buying decisions for their customers. Likewise, there are a growing number of knowledgeable,

independent wine consultants who provide expert advice to prospective purchasers.

What is the best strategy for an outlet to take in a wine auction purchase?
Most wine auctions these days take place online or as a live-online hybrid. For most professionals, we have found the best strategy is to set your maximum price and engage in absentee bidding. That is, have the auction house or bidding platform bid on your behalf. This way, a buyer is less likely to succumb to *auction fever* where the pursuit outweighs what would be a rational market value price for the wine of interest. All reputable auction houses offer this service at no charge to potential buyers.

Are there ever any bargains?
The great thing about wine auctions is that, if you are patient and diligent in your research, there are always bargains. A great strategy is to look beyond the big names and brands and focus on less heralded regions that are producing incredible quality wines. The wines of Spain, Australia and South America, as well as Oregon and Washington State, all fall into this category because they have historically underperformed at auction relative to their quality.

What are the typical charges above the 'hammer' price?
Because of the intense competition among the major auction houses, sellers are often charged little or no commissions, so auction houses rely on a *buyer's premium* for their revenue. This can range from 18-25% depending on the house. Shipping can range from $20 to $100 per case depending on the value of the wine, where it is coming from and where it is being shipped to. Always ask in advance what these charges would be. Depending on the jurisdiction involved, there may also be sales taxes applied. It is incumbent on the buyer to be aware of what regulations apply in their country, state or province. A good auction house will have this information at their fingertips and should never hesitate to offer relevant advice.

Who are the top auction houses in the wine business?
American-based auction houses continue to lead the market, although many have expanded into Hong Kong which serves as a clearinghouse for

the booming Asian market. Top auction houses include Acker, Zachys, Hart Davis Hart and Iron Gate (in Canada) as well as, of course, the more traditional international players of Sotheby's and Christie's.

What's up with expensive wines?
The fine wine market has been on a roll for the last ten years and even more so over the course of the pandemic. The Wine Market Journal's (WMJ150) index that functions much like major stock indices recorded 60% growth over the period of Q2 2020 to Q1 2022. Likewise, the London-based Cult Wine main investment index posted a net return to investors of 16% for 2021. Traditionally, fine wine collectors have generally skewed older; now there is a new, more demographically diverse group of collectors entering the market for both pleasure and investment purposes. Driving this demand is unsurpassed interest in Grand and Premier Cru wines from Burgundy, produced in relatively tiny quantities compared to the more traditional wines of Bordeaux that form the foundation of the market.

Have these top end wine prices affected the middle tiers?
The stratospheric prices for top wines such as Domaine de la Romanée-Conti (single bottles of the excellent 2002 vintage routinely trade for on average $26,000) have resulted in interest in a range of other producers of fine Burgundy such as Domaine Comte Georges de Vogüe and Domaine Armand Rousseau, which often trade in the mid-four figure range for good vintages. It has also impressed upon collectors that second, third and fourth growth wines from Bordeaux are a relative bargain, such as the excellent 2009 Château Cos d'Estournel from Saint-Estèphe which can be found on average to trade for about $300 per bottle.

We have heard that wines are counterfeited. Does this apply to all wines or only top products?
Again, it is important to deal only with reputable auction houses when purchasing fine wine. Yes, it is true that there are several counterfeit wines in the market and due diligence on the part of the auction house is key. Like in so many areas of the luxury goods sector, if something appears too good to be true, it likely is the case. Faked wines are still a relative rarity in the market, but unfortunately, they are not strictly limited to just

the super-high-end. There are a range of red flags to watch for including tampered labels, capsules or corks. The most important thing is to know who you are dealing with and never be afraid to ask questions from auction house specialists. It is their job to ensure that the products they offer are of unimpeachable provenance and authenticity.

Half Bottles but Not Half the Profits

There are many instances where a couple or group of two or three diners each want just a bit more than a glass of wine yet not a full bottle. The two of us refer to this situation by its scientific name of a 'midweek lunch', but others clearly have more on their proverbial plates and seldom have the time to sit around pondering life while slowing sipping down the entire 750 milliliters (25.4 ounces for those readers in the United States, Liberia and Myanmar).

The problem with this goldilocks zone is that carrying a proper armada of wines by the glass would result in a ton of spoilage. Enter the half bottle which lets bars and restaurants dole out well over a standard five ounce pour per head from a freshy uncorked vintage, leaving everyone at the table satisfied while opening more of the menu to such a flexible, middle ground purchase.

From the restaurant manager's perspective, the first key advantage of half bottles is that the margins can be higher than BTG purchases. As a lot of the costs to the restaurant are packaging, this isn't necessarily the case when compared to full bottles or magnums, though, depending on how these scales are priced. From the customer's point of view, a bevy of half bottles opens the doors to substantially more variety as two or three different vintages can be sampled during a single sitting.

Besides being more expensive on a per-ounce basis than their full bottle counterparts, for disadvantages, limited availability comes to mind. Many wineries just don't offer them. Next – and this one is a subtle one – some servers somehow struggle to open half bottles, which hurts the overall presentation and casts a subconscious feeling of nonconfidence over the whole ordeal.

Incorporating half bottles into your wine list is an artform that great restaurant managers and sommeliers must handle on a vintage-by-vintage basis. Should the same product be offered in both half and full bottles? This depends on who the clientele is and how quickly your inventory moves. A second issue that many don't consider until it's too late is that some cellars or wine storage units can't accommodate half bottles; their slender shapes ensures that they slip through the holsters.

All doubts aside, opportunities abound, foremost in the realm of desserts – Sauternes, Tokaji from Hungary or ice wines from Ontario as three options. Given one's reduced tolerance for sweet things, dessert wines often come in a smaller 200mL or 6.7 ounce bottle, making them perfect for a table to explore as part of an extended, multi-course dinner. As well, some Champagne houses offer half bottles or splits, generally around 187mL or 6.3 ounces, yet one more avenue for complementing great food with the right beverage proportion.

Stocking a Region's Signature Grape

While most oenophiles can recite a litany of grape varietals and their traits off the cuff, most consumers aren't nearly as informed. They've likely heard of the top international grapes that have been transplanted around the globe as well as one or two that characterize a specific region, but beyond that getting into esoteric vintages can be both intimidating as well as alluring.

Thus, by knowing what's common knowledge and what isn't, you can guide your inventory to be more congruent with your restaurant's strategic vision to thereby increase beverage revenues and meal satisfaction. First, let's look at some examples of what we mean by signature grape, sorted by country or region:

- *Argentina:* Malbec
- *Australia:* Shiraz (for reds at least)
- *Austria:* Grüner Veltliner (for whites)
- *Burgundy:* Chardonnay, Pinot Noir and Gamay (otherwise known as Beaujolais)
- *California:* Chardonnay and Cabernet Sauvignon
- *Chile:* Caménère
- *Germany:* Riesling and Gewürztraminer (for whites)

- *Greece:* Assyrtiko and Xinomavro
- *New Zealand:* Sauvignon Blanc (for whites)
- *Oregon:* Pinot Noir
- *Piedmont:* Nebbiolo (the varietal used in the prestigious Barolo or Barbaresco)
- *Spain:* Tempranillo and Garnacha (for reds)
- *Tuscany:* Sangiovese (and its most popular production into Chianti)

Signature grapes matter when you think about them in terms of customer expectations. For instance, suppose you operate a traditional Italian trattoria with a flair for Tuscan dishes such as (our favorite) Bistecca Fiorentina. When the average guest first sees the wine list, the expectation from the above bullet points would be to see some Chiantis and other expressions of Sangiovese – two being Vino Nobile di Montepulciano and Super Tuscans which are often around 80-90% of this varietal.

Imagine a patron's surprise, though, if the wine list doesn't include these anticipated offerings or only a paltry selection. Unconsciously, it makes the decision process harder due to the inherent unfamiliarity with what's written on the page, introducing an ounce of apprehension. This lack of confidence in turn can deter the sale of more expensive vintages and result in fewer bottles or glasses sold overall.

On the other hand, if the branding and theme of the restaurant is to be avant-garde and playing against stereotypes, then it would make perfect sense for the wine list to be equally as edgy and unpredictable. In such cases, the operator can temper any patron anxiety over not knowing what to expect in a wine purchase through server education and perhaps some written cues on the menu such as what the more obscure varietals are known for, some tasting notes or even a little story about the winery.

There is no one-size-fits-all solution for whether you go with the flow of customers' preformed beliefs about what each region produces or aim to subvert those expectations. The latter can serve your restaurant by helping create a more surprising, and thus memorable, dining experience because you're different, but it can also result in fewer bottles sold if you aren't supporting this counterintuitive approach with the right signals that will imbue some semblance of comfort.

The most important action you can take is to know your outlet's *raison d'être* or 'reason of being'. Are you servicing people who are primarily looking for a no-frills meal with just a bit of flair? Or does your outlet strive to attract more special occasion guests who are seeking you out specifically for a culinary adventure? Knowing this core direction will then give you a clearer answer to guide the wine list and how to stock a region's signature grapes.

Wine Lists and QR-Coded Menus Don't Mix

A whole book on proper menu design could be written that's specific to wine lists, and needless to say that inventory arrangements, fonts, graphics, spacing, types of paper, menu backings and all other stylistic concerns do in fact matter when it comes to influencing patrons to buy one bottle versus another, or to convince them to buy a bottle in the first place over going by the glass.

The pandemic has thrown a wrench in this process as many customers now expect menus to be accessible on their phones via a QR (quick ready) code. The benefit for the restaurant is certainly there in the form of saving on printing costs, but it's nonetheless a tradeoff.

Paper is palpable. You feel the slight roughness of a thick paper stock, subtly smell the ink, are delighted by the way the room's lighting creates soft shadows on the page and are soothed by (what we ideally hope that you would use for your establishment) the touch of the leather menu backing on the palm of your hand.

Viewing a wine list on your phone gives you none of those sensations. Yes, you get graphics, color and the ability to keep the webpage updated in real-time as inventory changes with no additional costs, but everything beyond the straight visuals are lost in the endless scroll of a two-dimensional screen.

And building on this notion of scrolling, one critical difference is that a physical list – or even a binder in the case for some restaurants with an expansive cellar – presents all bottles together for readers to consider, whereas a responsive webpage (over simply displaying a PDF version of the menu) will usually configure all items into a single column to keep everything legible and to avoid lots of pinching.

The problem here is one of perception, where a narrowly focused column viewed off of one's phone can increase the observed length of the wine list, resulting in patrons 'dropping off' before perusing the entirety of it. Hence, if you're hoping for guests to land on those top-shelf vintages at the end of your list, forget about it as they'll barely make it through the BTG offerings.

While the psychological issue of physical versus digital menu is one that will continue to evolve as the long tail of the pandemic plays out, one consideration for the here and now is to bifurcate the BTG list from the full list of vintages. Then it comes down to knowing your customer. When two friends plunk down at the bar and don't order any food, chances are they'll be vastly more inclined to go BTG, have a pint or ring up a cocktail than to split a full bottle. On the other hand, a couple that's looking for a proper three-course dinner will stand a far better chance of wanting to complement that special occasion meal will a great bottle of wine to elevate the experience.

For this latter cohort, presenting the optionality is perfectly acceptable through questions like, "Wine by the glass is available via the regular beverage menu accessible by scanning the QR code at your table, but would you want us to bring over the full wine list for you to select a bottle?" Have a rough idea of how your customer is thinking and that's how you'll maximize wine sales.

Sizing Up Your Somm

So far, we've talked about varietals, vintages, pairings, wine list design, growing regions, price points, rating systems, glassware and touched on a smattering of tips for training or motivating servers. But we haven't addressed what you should look for when evaluating a sommelier, generally referred to as a somm.

These cellar masters can be a tremendous value-add to the team and your beverage revenues, on top of their fiduciary responsibility of managing the inventory. Whoever you hire will likely be tasked with purchasing, pricing, maintaining supplier or wholesaler relationships and wine list development. There's also a ton of collaboration with the executive chef and restaurant manager on programs, promotions and pairings to help elevate the restaurant's renown.

What criteria do you look for in a great sommelier? After a background check, there are professional qualifications that must be met, specifically the three levels offered by the Court of Master Sommeliers or Wine & Spirit Education Trust (WSET), along with a series of specialty courses for specific producing nations and other diplomas in spirits or sake. At a minimum, a somm candidate should have passed the WSET second level, although any serious dining establishment should consider a third level and perhaps a Master of Wine designation to add real credibility to help sell those thousand-dollar vintages.

That's the technical and back-of-house side of things, though. The greatest success factor for a sommelier will inevitable be their ability to work directly with customers. Consider questions like:

- How do they size up a customer and recommend the right wine?
- How do they present the wine, both physically as well as verbally?
- How do they describe the wine's taste?
- How do they refer to the various grape types as well as the relationship with wine and food?
- How do they carry a conversation?
- How do they handle objections?

In essence, this echoes one of the core hiring principles for any hospitality role. *You can always train a skill, but you can never train for passion.* All the questions above relate to soft skills, yet to develop them a somm needs an innate drive. They must inherently want to serve the guest by ensuring the wine selection is optimized to their preferred dining experience.

We have interviewed candidates for this position as part of our hotel asset management duties over the years, and the first ingredient we look for is a die-hard passion for wine. A great sommelier not only appreciates the $75 bottles that everyone else under the sun is bound to enjoy but also has a soft spot for those $20 gems.

Our interviews are always interactive, asking prospects to describe a wine, open it, taste it and comment. Like a chef who always bring their own knives, the best candidates also carry their own corkscrews (with extra points for having a Forge de Laguiole on hand). We also touch on their wine philosophy, specific vintage preferences and selling techniques.

What's making this hiring process fun is that alcohol consumption is not just allowed but mandatory for every interview. If you heed the above tips, you will know the right candidate when you meet them.

Don't Forget Your Waitstaff

Many restaurants do not have a sommelier. Or, if they do, there may be shifts where that position is not filled – midday lunches, for example. What do you do with your waitstaff? What is the best approach to motivating your team to develop a passion for wine to maximize revenues?

Particularly in a labor crunch, your team is likely harried, working overtime and possibly burnt out. You must make their lives easier so that they aren't rushed or distracted when tableside. Put yourself in their shoes. What can you do to help them so that the passion shines through?

Start with the wine list. If you don't have a somm to answer complex questions nor the time to train your team, you should aim to keep it simple. Cover the main grape types and key regions; you don't have to cover the world. Focus on the big, well-worked countries like France, Italy and the United States. Then add basic descriptions to each listing that novice wine drinkers can comprehend like light, full-bodied or semi-sweet.

Part of simplicity also means limiting selection; it makes no sense to have multiple variations of the same varietal or vintage. By the glass options are great, too. Keep the price points clustered, eliminating the subconscious primer for a decision to be made from a significant price spread in lieu of adequate substantiation for the more expensive choice. Wine recommendations for mains printed onto the menu also work to reduce the burden on your team to do the selling.

Next, when it comes to your waitstaff, training is inescapable for wine. Show them how to properly use a corkscrew (as well as how to elegantly handle the screw tops!) and what the key elements of wine tasting are. Explain what wines go best with certain dishes and some basic problem solving to address basic questions asked by patrons.

Most wholesalers will offer and lead wine education sessions on their wines. Arrange these as they are not only good for learning and sales, but they are also fun team gatherings to boost morale. Just be sure to repeat the training on a regular basis – perhaps quarterly – to reinforce the knowledge and particularly when your wine menu changes. To this end, keep cheat sheets in the kitchen or behind the bar with tasting notes on every popular wine sold. When in doubt, let a server defer to a bartender who is likely to have a bit more wherewithal about the beverages sold versus just the food.

The third broad suggestion is to be creative. For instance, develop an insert sheet for your menu that shows the wine label and some descriptive information so that people can look it up on your phones or defer to a wine-specific app like Vivino. For this, it's all about taking the load off your increasingly busy team and adding a bit of interactivity to nudge the purchase.

You may even consider a team tasting event amongst your waitstaff, letting them taste the difference between various wines sold, then rewarding the winners with bottles. Again, it's all about motivation and keeping spirits high to prevent employee churn. Such simple adjustments can and do go a long way.

TALES FROM THE TERROIR

Upselling from a Glass to a Bottle

As we are writing this, we are in the midst of an economic downturn. While employment levels remain high, there is a high degree of uncertainty. This in turn can be disastrous for your restaurant's alcohol sales – takeout or dine-in whenever that returns – because customers will have less disposable cash to spend lavishly.

But rather than simply abstaining from liquor altogether, what we may observe on a cheque-by-cheque basis is that patrons opt for wine by the glass in lieu of purchasing a whole bottle. Besides a cost comparison, let's look at five other motivating factors for why someone would go BTG to hopefully come up with some counterpoints so that your cellar sales don't suffer.

1. Wine lists have become increasingly unwieldy, complex to manage and intimidating to the average guest who isn't conversant enough in the lingo to know what's good value.
2. Related to this, many customers may feel uneasy when asking a wine steward or sommelier as they feel that they are being sold a product at an inflate price or are being steered toward a slow mover.
3. Often diners choose diametrically opposite mains – think salmon for one and pepper steak for the other – which makes pairing with a single wine quite untenable.
4. Similarly, members of a group may be inflexible in their alcohol preferences or looking to sample several offerings, making consensus difficult.
5. Drinking and driving is a constant concern, with one glass enjoyed during a meal acceptable while a whole bottle consumed may be pushing the limit.

To these points above, not all can be addressed with a single remedy, but there are nevertheless ways to prompt bottle sales even in a bear market. Here are some approaches to consider:

- Simplifying your total wine inventory will help to narrow a customer's field of view so that *shopper's paralysis* becomes less of an issue. This will take some work in the transition where you must incentivize guests to get rid of your undesirable stock or reallocate some to banquet orders. And you may want to also examine how anchor pricing'\ can help to make expensive labels more attractive.

- Developing trust between your servers or somm and your patrons requires a lot of training, but it also calls for a lot of work to reframe the dining experience before customers arrive. Use your owned marketing channels to build the narrative that your restaurant is a purveyor of a well-curated selection and that your team is fully knowledgeable in all entries. Host staff tastings if need be or build a 'sommelier's choice' section to highlight seasonal favorites.

- Training will also help your team to navigate the many individual preferences within a group so that a compromise can be found. Again, limiting the total selection can in many ways lead to greater flexibility as it lets guests see the full range of options rather than revert to what they already know due to the *paradox of choice* problem. If anything, your team should understand general tendencies for appetizers versus mains so that the bottles chosen can follow the food.

- Watching a corked bottle be opened tableside is entertaining and adds to the dining experience. While many are trending towards the twist-off tops, we would personally avoid these as they cheapen the show and have a lower perceived value.

- New technologies such as cellar apps can give you a laser focus on inventory numbers so that you have more accurate insights on what's moving and what isn't. Plus, if these apps have a guest-facing version, then you can better connect your inventory to the web so that you can still facilitate sales in as touchless a manner as possible.

Off-Color Wines Sell Big

An age-old expression that any good chef knows is that people also eat with their eyes. As any manager who runs a successful cocktail bar can also attest, the same is true for beverages, and we can apply this principle to enhance wine sales.

While taste and smell are always paramount for any bottle, the color of a wine can unconsciously influence someone's perception of that vintage and heighten satisfaction with that choice. Moreover, a wine's extraordinary color can be utilized as either a written or on-the-spot sales motivator.

This brings us to off-color wines. Think whites made from a spectrum of common varietals that can be described as having an orange, amber or burnt gold hue. Next, Grüner Veltliner from Austria and Vinho Verde from Portugal are renowned for their chartreuse coloring. Some Pinot Noirs can even be so light they have a semitransparent scarlet-ruby tint. Contrast this with a well-made Vino Nobile di Montepulciano which are quintessentially violet or a Sagrantino di Montefalco that edge towards inky black. Finally, one could even argue that the entire surge of rosé sales in the past couple decades is a direct result of these wines' brilliant array of watermelon, strawberry, salmon and tangerine colorations, fitting with the 'millennial pink' craze.

Examples abound for labels that don't fit into the standard white and red molds. While anyone who knows their wine would never judge a bottle based solely upon its label design or the liquid's color, sommeliers and oenophiles represent only a small percentage of the population. And even still, a wine's color is a factor in any formalized scoring system.

This leaves us with the average consumer who is likely to be marginally versed in their wine knowledge with novice taste buds to boot. Say you put five whites in front of a wine rookie, and all are the same yellow color save for one that has some cloudy bronze shading. Do you think that, without any real depth of vinicultural knowledge, this individual will perceive the off-color glass to be better than the rest or in the top two? At the very least, they may be intrigued.

While we often leave cellar orders to the sommelier or restaurateur who has several decades of drinking and studying alcoholic beverages under their belt, this can instill a disconnect with your patrons because they don't experience wine the same way you do. This is often called the *curse of knowledge*. But customers don't necessarily care about structure, tannins, terroir, blending percentages or any other jargon. Most of the time, they just want something that tastes good from a varietal that they are already somewhat familiar with and one that pairs well with their food.

We've had to deal with this scenario firsthand when helping oversee the development of a wine list as part of a dining outlet relaunch at a resort where we acted as the asset managers. To resolve this disconnect, we organized a full day where ourselves, the sommelier, the general manager and the marketing director all got together then met with a series of merchants to sample and rate their products. As part of this process, one criterion we ranked wines on was their coloration with an x-factor allowance for ones that were visual standouts – be it a vibrant hue, opacity or nice wine tears. Importantly, we wanted someone with marketing knowledge to be present to offer a differing opinion on what might appeal to the more novice guests.

After sampling six-dozen wines (and staying sober by using the spittoon!), we tallied the results and made a note to have a full range of colors for the BTG menu. At launch, this proved to be a highly successful tactic to boost wine revenues as our servers were armed with a simple and swift tool to help sell. If you are undecided and don't have the appetite for more wine knowledge, then don't worry about where it's from or its vintage; just pick a color.

The gist of this story is to know that people drink with their eyes and plan the dining experience accordingly. This, of course, also pertains to the décor, lighting and general ambiance, but if you have an opportunity to market a bottle based upon its noteworthy coloring (or any other truly exceptional quality for that matter), then you should definitely explore it.

The Wines of Summer

While most wines can be enjoyed any time of year and ostensibly anywhere within sight of a corkscrew, the hot summer months present an opportunity to expand your beverage selection with great seasonal offerings. While the meetings with vendors, tastings, procurement, shipping of new cases and printing of new menus can all take place inside of a month, the strategic vision needs an equal amount of time or longer to properly gestate.

With the proverbial line in the sand for patio season occurring in the United States around the Memorial Day long weekend (Victoria Day weekend for Canadians), if you start thinking about the theme in spring then you will have given yourself a full month to research and ruminate on the best concept as well as give your senior team enough time for input before signoff. You need a few weeks for some deliberate thought with the hope that you can conjure up the one big idea that will generate buzz and distinguish your wine list, beer list or cocktail collection. For inspiration, spend some time meandering through social media to see what other restaurants or hobbyists are doing. Then look to start small with a singular, punchy concept that you can execute and execute well.

Let's focus solely on wine and how it relates to this season, of which top of mind is rosé, now a summer staple with far more than plonk at your disposal. Renowned for their drinkability, such wines can range from headache sweet to savory dry, with colors from shimmering amber and blush watermelon to deep cherry red. All are delightfully enjoyable when chilled while some also deliver an amusing bouquet and plenty of ripe fruit at warmer temperatures.

With so much at your disposal if you so choose to go this route, instead of just announcing your rosé inventory and listing off these specials on a menu insert, it's a matter of embellishing such a program. Do you organize your list by price, by taste profile, by place of origin or by color? If a group orders a full bottle, what accoutrements, like a nicely polished bucket brimming with ice, does the server present with it?

A small step away from rosé would be whites and sparkling wines like Prosecco. The trend for both when discussed in relation to the sweltering heat of June, July and August is towards lighter, less sweet concoctions that refresh the palate or offer a counterbalance to traditional outdoor cuisine. Perhaps your summer program could be a white and seafood special.

Both types of wines have grown leaps and bounds in nearly every production region in the world, so finding a great local or semi-local offering shouldn't be a chore. What we would emphasize if you embarked down this path is that you stray away from those brands that are well-stocked in the nearby bottle shop as they won't offer your patrons anything extraordinary or memorable in the overall experience.

Segueing into beer, the classics for summer are the lightly hopped wheat varieties. With the craft beer scene now firmly entrenched in every hipster denizen, it won't be hard to find one or two that could fulfill the local quota. Or look for a few niche European imports. Remember your presentation, as one nice flourish for a wheat beer might be to serve each glass with a decoratively sliced orange wedge.

Also hot on the scene are ciders, sour ales, shandies and radlers. Just imagine if you had a wild-fermented cider program that also included a few growlers for groups. Make it engaging and entertaining, and you'll surely move a ton of inventory come summer.

Designing the Perfect Wine Tasting

While you may already have an outstanding wine list that adroitly runs the gamut from approachable, BTG labels to those sticker-stock, special-occasion bottles, it is nonetheless advisable that you tack on a flight or tasting program so that you can meet this modern demand. Here a few pointers when designing such an experience:

Quality Over Quantity: This harks back to the concept of the paradox of choice whereby when you give someone too many options and too much information to digest all at once, deciding or even processing all the various micro-experiences becomes intimidating and stressful. While this is hardly a push for keeping it simple, your tasting must have a structure so that guests can properly form the narrative in their minds.

Presentation Matters: If a wine tasting isn't posted to social media, did it ever even happen? Such is the world we will live in nowadays, but rather than scoff at it you would be better off adapting to the times. Think in terms of moments prime for Instagram. Presentation affects nearly every attribute of the experience – the glassware, the table setting, the room décor, the lighting, the way the food is placed on the plate and the way a wine tasting is framed by the team.

Nontraditional Complements: Everyone has an ingrained image in their heads of wine paired with cheese and perhaps a few crackers or dried fruit on the side. Add an element of surprise by offering an unexpected meal accompaniment ranging from olives, house-smoked meats, tomatoes or nuts to dessert samplings, marinated seafood and artisanal breads with homemade spreads. Anything that can pair is fair game.

Hyper-Regionality: As an extension of the movements for local and authentic dining, this neologism for our oenophilic purposes would inscribe a very narrow focus on one particular commune or microclimate to tell a holistic story about that area. An example from a trip to Tuscany, hyper-regionality would focus on a specific valley or commune rather than provide a smattering from towns that may be hours apart from each other. Based on a visit to Montepulciano, a tasting from only this town might include a Rosso, Vino Nobile, Reserva and a Grappa to finish off, complemented by a few different Pecorinos from the neighboring city of Pienza. All would be produced within a 25-kilometer radius. Sourcing would be a consummate issue for something of this caliber, but the result is that you are giving your guests a memory that will last a lifetime.

Knowledgeable Guides: Ideally you would have each flight immaculately prepared and described by the sommelier or a veteran server. Regardless, training is a must, as part of the experience will always be the human factor – the positive attitude your team brings to the occasion and how well they are able to address questions to enhance the self-actualization aspect. If staffing is an issue or if demand outpaces server availability, you will need to prepare some literature so that patrons can embark upon a self-directed tasting. Such pamphlets or web-based descriptions should be fun but also educational, and they should give some semblance of instructions as to how best to savor each component.

Souvenirs: Offering your guests a keepsake will give them one extra surprise to help solidify the memory over the long-term. The most obvious form of a leave-behind would be an embroidered copy of the tasting menu. Another easy one would be house-crafted, gift-wrapped desserts of any kind; a few chocolate truffles or profiteroles should suffice. Beyond that, get creative and make sure that the souvenir stays on theme.

Mini Tastings: An elaborate tasting of any sort typically commands a somewhat exclusionary price tag just for the restaurant to recover its costs. How can you compress the experience down to something that can be enjoyed on a whim and only lasts for a maximum of 15 minutes of entertainment? Think no more than three wines in one or two ounce pours and three different snacks as accompaniments. Just because of its abbreviated format is no reason not to have it follow a given theme and tell a meaningful story.

Continual Innovation: Nothing is every truly perfect, but we can always strive to get ever closer by tweaking, tinkering and trying new things. Ask your guests for firsthand feedback and listen to what your team has heard. See what's working and what might need a further dose of creativity. You may also want to adjust tastings based on the inventory and what older stock you are trying to get rid of in advance of new seasonal orders.

Beverage Specialist Nomenclature

Many restaurants already encourage staff education and even more waiters see this as an avenue for bigger tips; basic wine knowledge has become the norm rather than a value-add. And therein lies yet one more opportunity.

This doesn't mean you should abort all attempts at staff education or in offering recommendations. Rather, we have to put our marketing caps on for a moment to see if there's a way we can tweak this aspect of the meal experience so that it feels fresh again. And an easy solution may be in further specializing your restaurant team by giving these dedicated experts uniquely alluring and fun titles.

The inspiration that sparked this concept came about tangentially when discussing a somewhat recent initiative at select Ritz-Carlton alpine resorts where they have introduced a 'smoreologist' which is, in essence, a fancy name for a pastry chef who experiments with fancy graham crackers and marshmallows. The name resonates, though, helping create some excitement amongst the family crowd or at least a hearty chuckle.

For wine and from the guest's perspective, it's one thing for a suggestion to come from a waiter while it's a whole other level for it to come from a sommelier. Regardless of whether the wine recommendation is better, official accreditations imply trust. Thus, any sort of in-house labor specialization or professional designation you can implement will help to augment the meal experience. Choose a title and build a program around a designated team member.

It makes sense for a fine dining establishment with a massive wine cellar to have a sommelier. In fact, you would probably be suspicious if they didn't have one. On the food front, an affineur on staff is a wise choice if you offer a wide variety of cheeses. Likewise, the smoreologist example fits the bill because of the resort's mountain lodge setting while elevating your pastry chef to chocolatier will go over well with the chocoholics amongst us.

Other examples include a cicerone for a brewpub or microbrewery attached to your restaurant. Ditto 'whiskey expert' for those establishments with a substantial number of top shelf bottles on display. Next are bartenders with a bit of craft who are now called mixologists. If you have a prominent tea program, then advance one of your team members as your 'tea sommelier' or 'tea specialist'. Similarly, while you may already have a dedicated barista on staff, do you have a 'coffee master' who can not only roast a mean bean but can also speak eloquently about said coffee's country of origin, the brewing process, specific aromas and tasting notes?

It's all a matter of devoting some energy to further expounding upon what you already do best, and then using clever nomenclature as a marketing tactic. We've noted a few naming combinations in the paragraph above as well as some ubiquitous modifier words like 'specialist' or 'master', but there are others to consider like consultant, connoisseur, aficionado, maestro (perhaps best for restaurants with a diverse array of Italian liquors), gourmand, ambassador (too United Nations sounding for our liking) or even feinschmecker, an unfamiliar yet appropriate German word to denote a gourmand.

Elevating the Mixologist

With so much focus on wine, we may be neglecting the potential for cocktails to help differentiate your brand. Additionally, there are many customers who consider mixed drinks an essential part of a restaurant's identity and will specifically seek out or recommend such places based upon these offerings. Much like how you promote your executive chef to boost the profile of your restaurants, you must now also become an impresario for your bar staff.

To rewind about two or three decades, consider the first generation of this evolution as the position of head bartender morphed into the more scientific-sounding role of mixologist. While not quite at the same level as the sommelier – which has an actual accreditation – such individuals have done wonders to integrate dynamic and inspirational beverages into what restaurants can offer to guests.

Now that that title has become mainstream, however, it isn't perking brows like it used to. And so, it's time to innovate once again. A few clever marketers have put on their neologism hats to conjure up a few more tongue-in-cheek iterations to keep customers buying those $20+ cocktails. As four relatively simple expressions of this, think 'executive mixologist', 'celebrity mixologist', 'beverage curator' and 'cocktail consultant'. We've even seen the term 'farm to bar' used in some eateries where local sourcing is mandated for practically all cocktail ingredients.

Some of these terms will sound more professional while others will be fun and perhaps a little cheeky. All the while, such distinctions and loftier titles will help you to command higher prices without guests feeling slighted, but only if the end results fit with the story. That is, if you are going to designate someone as an executive mixologist as a way of differentiating your restaurant, they better not just craft any plain Old Fashioned. Challenge your team to spend some time creating a truly exceptional cocktail menu, and then see if they are worthy of an extraordinary job title.

Skunked Wine as Service Excellence

This is one of the worst feelings in the world. You pop open a bottle, pour yourself a glass, take a sip and your mouth is hit by a musty, astringent splash that eviscerates any other flavors. The wine is skunked and utterly worthless.

However, in a hospitality capacity, corked bottles can serve as an opportunity to wow your patrons. It all comes down to one of the hallmarks of a great service culture in that it's not just about how well you provide for your guests but also how well you recover from any errors or experiential gaps, with the term *double deviations* epitomizing this principle.

The biggest worry about a bottle going stale is that you never can tell until it's opened. Of course, you can make assumptions based on the winery, varietal and vintage, but it's still always a question mark. A litmus test of sorts before you even let a guest take a sip is to sniff the wet end of the cork. The aroma will, as per the title, obviously have skunky elements, while other telltale signs of decay are any notes of wood, mold, manure, barnyard, hay, potato skins or asparagus. If you have never encountered a corked bottle, you'll know it when you smell it!

The taste will follow in stride and more strongly than the funky fragrance, but if the smell is palpably wrong, the last thing you want to then do is let a guest endure the displeasure of having even one sip. Right there, just with a simply whiff, is the chance for your servers to demonstrate their knowledge and deepen their rapport with customers. There are also other visual signs to note so that your team can best service their patrons by preventing them from tasting a skunked drop, including the liquor having a brownish, opaque color, a fizzy structure when it's not a sparkling wine or perhaps the cork is pushed out slightly from the neck.

Regardless of when or how the rot is discovered, what matters most is what your server does next. The most basic form of follow-up is to go back to the cellar, pull out another bottle of the same label and open it to see if it too is off. In all likelihood it'll taste just fine. However, you must keep in mind that by this point the table has been waiting for its drinks for an additional five to ten minutes, delaying the regular course of the collective meal experience and letting frustration set in to reduce overall meal satisfaction.

A little something extra is needed to balance the books, even if the deterioration of flavors was in no way your restaurant's fault. The fact remains that guests will perceive this as a slight on your part and they are thus justified in their nonverbal desires for a gratis gift for their troubles. While we're not suggesting you comp the entire purchase, a free dessert or an extra round at the end of the meal will go a long way to both positively surprising a table and build even more advocacy for your restaurant than if everything had gone smoothly from the start.

Two times this has happened to us at a restaurant. The first was at Gordon Ramsay Steakhouse in Paris Las Vegas where we ordered a bottle of 2000 Clos de Vougeot. The sommelier tasted it before us– the correct approach – and promptly rejected the bottle before bringing out a second bottle of the same wine, which was perfect.

The second was at Champlain Restaurant in the Fairmont Le Château Frontenac in Québec City where we ordered a bottle of Fixin Premier Cru, an above average burgundy. This time the sommelier poured the wine for us to taste, and when we remarked that it was terrible; he too tasted it then concurred that it was off. Afraid to bring out another bottle of the same wine, he upgraded us to a grand cru of an even better year for no additional charge. Although the recovery incentive was better for the latter incident, what's remarkable is that, despite both incidents occurring years ago, the adept handling of events is still quite memorable.

The key here is that whenever there is a fault, your recovery efforts must be speedy and forthright. And instead of leaving these types of situations up to the moment whereby a manager is forced to decide extemporaneously, set up a protocol in advance for how to best compensate guests for their troubles.

Wine Ratings as a Double-Edged Sword

While 100-point wines command a universal and unquestionably level of prestige that any hotel would be happy to have, the same cannot necessarily be said for 90 or even 95-point bottles. Understanding where to deploy a ranking can help build your restaurant revenues, but only if you proceed cautiously.

What we have noticed over the past decade is a form of scope creep whereby numeric ratings are steadily appearing within more and more wine lists or advertisements, becoming a foundational aspect of any customer presentation. The problem here is that rankings are a spice, not a main ingredient; too much can destroy a dish and too many different rating services can dilute the overall impact of the number itself.

Wine ratings first reached mass appeal through Robert Parker in the mid-1970s via his newsletter, *The Wine Advocate.* Using a 50 to 100-point scale, he set out to independently appraise wines and in doing so became the most popular and influential critic. As an example, his ratings became a primary driver of pricing for each newly released Bordeaux vintage.

Today, there are thousands if not millions of wines available globally. Thus, it is impossible for any one individual to evaluate enough to satisfy the expanding consumer demand. There are also many more critics, among the most popular are *Wine Spectator, Wine Enthusiast, Vinous* and several other well-known independents. Most use the 100-point scale established by Robert Parker. Chances are that some of the wines you are buying from your distributors have been rated, with scores generally in the range of 88 to 94 and rarely higher.

In addition to numeric ratings there are also wine competitions that issue medals, although these are often executed on a more local level with the results quite variable from event to event and from year to year. Wineries and wine merchants will often flag all this information as part of their sales pitch to help move product.

Importantly for you, what does this all mean and how do you use these ratings? First, the information has value to your customer, at least for now. It provides reassurance that the wine has been identified by some critic or organization that has deemed it better than plonk. Remember, though, that a 90 by one party does not necessarily mean the wine is inferior to a 91 by another.

Second, you can use these ratings to drum up sales and increase beverage satisfaction by adjoining them to the wine listed on your menu. But for transparency, always mention the name of the rating agency or critic as your source, while also verifying that the number correctly aligns with the vintage in your cellar.

Thirdly, and as an asterisk to the second point, educate your staff on the ratings and their value. Everyone on your team must understand that they are just educated opinions and that the unrated wines are not necessarily inferior.

Therein lies the double-edged sword. Does having a numeric rating beside one label detract from selling other bottles that don't have numbers next to them? Taken to the extreme, if you were to list ratings for all wines in your cellar, would this become an issue of too much information to thus induce shopper's paralysis?

On a macro-level, with so many different ranking systems emerging, does this weaken the power of the 100-point scale itself? We argue it does. When every magazine, website and distributor have their own recommendations under Robert Parker's general guidelines, the number itself loses value in the eyes of the customer because they don't have time to verify the competence of the rater that bestows a 90 or 95 to a wine.

As the adage goes, it's too much of a good thing. Hence, the best course is to use wine ratings sparingly and only convey highly trusted sources like those abovementioned. Alternatively, instead of typing any numbers into the menu, if you trust your servers, you can arm them with some points for certain wines then let them disclose this information when asked by a table.

Hybrid Restaurant and Retail Spaces for Wine Sales

Traditionally, the selling pathway for wine is to usher customers to the table, let them glance over the menu before ordering or making a recommendation, then deliver drinks or a full bottle. Sometimes, though, you can run against the curve for heightened interactivity and revenues.

This brings us to our triumphant return to Las Vegas – the first trip back following the pandemic lockdowns – where we stayed Resorts World Las Vegas and wandered over to the hotel's Wally's franchise (the original being in Los Angeles), a high-end cheese, charcuterie, wine and spirits retail store as well as a fantastic restaurant. What's of note here is that anything on display in the store can be bought via a 'cash and carry' point of sale, then taken away or consumed on premise at the restaurant for only a nominal corkage fee (currently) of $40.

As essentially a luxury grab-and-go outlet, what elevates Wally's is its well-curated collection of wine, spirits and accoutrement combined with upscale décor to complete the atmosphere. Equally impressive were the bundles which assembled one, two or sometimes three bottles as well as selected chocolate or other snack pairings, and all for a reasonable price considering it's on The Strip.

How might this apply to your restaurant? Would you consider going with a retail-restaurant hybrid remodeling?

To start, you must be cognizant of the evolving nature of the restaurant business. Think upscale casual dining, food halls, online ordering apps, lounge-style seating arrangements and the aforementioned grab-and-go setup. Two themes throughout this evolution are greater convenience and flexibility. Pivoting to a hybrid setup may be a viable means of revitalizing a sluggish space.

Still, there are lots of issues. Foremost are costs of conversion, how the new price points may affect sales margins, how this model may affect turns and what to stock or bundle to heighten guest revenues. Next are the legalities over selling alcohol in a grab-and-go manner. Las Vegas is perhaps one of the most pliable municipalities, but it won't hurt to inquire as many of the previous restrictions have been dispatched as an ongoing means of supporting the struggling restaurant industry.

As we've remarked numerous times before, wine is as much about the flavor of the beverage as it is the ambiance within which it is imbibed. Adding a store-like experience to your restaurant represents one way to imbue that dynamic sense of flexibility.

Lessons from Eataly

We've been to Chicago and New York City dozens of times before, and the Eataly store locations in both cities have been on our list since their respective openings. During a recent four-hour stopover in Chicago, we had time to do two things: have lunch with friends traveling for work and visit the titular Italo-foodie nexus.

Founded by the Italian entrepreneur, Oscar Farinetti, in 2007, Eataly takes a William Sonoma approach to grocery shopping whereby high-end products and fancy, spacious displays trump the need to pack every available shelf. They serve food as well; the two-story space we toured had a Lavazza café, gelateria and a Nutella waffle kiosk on the main floor with formal seating areas and bars mixed in between the grocery aisle on the mezzanine.

For those who haven't graced the halls of an Eataly franchise, make plans for a lengthy sojourn when you are next in Boston, Chicago, Los Angeles, Las Vegas, New York, Toronto or practically any major Italian city. You can easily spend two hours bouncing between the wine section, the hundreds of cheeses, the packaged goods and all the compiled cookbooks.

What fascinated us most about Eataly is that the store takes an educational approach to grocery shopping, thereby adding new dimensions and depth to the customer experience. In store, there are maps – one for truffle picking by season, the other for grape varietals by growing region. What is apparent from these maps is how they both serve to visually convey the great geographic diversity of Italian produce.

How many of you know the difference between white and black truffles, and the best time of year to visit certain provinces of Italy to partake in the annual traditional of truffle picking? We didn't, but after perusing the store's maps, we had a better sense of what the answer is. Moreover, it got us curious; we wanted to learn more. It's the little 'did you know' moments that stimulate patrons' minds in a different way than the sights, sounds, smells and tastes.

Nowadays, there is a strong demand for food awareness and education beyond simply serving a fascinating meal with equally excellent service. People want to know where ingredients are coming from, what their health benefits are and how the cuisine is prepared. It's this same principle that helps explain the rising popularity of restaurants with kitchens that face onto their diners; customers can see every part of the cooking process. Further, look at market-style food shopping. It's not just a matter of pulling stuff off the shelves but being able to converse with the vendor in order to guide your end purchase.

How can we apply this 'Eatalian' lesson to your restaurant and your wine list? Simple: it's also about paying the knowledge forward. Educate your servers about the food and wine that are offered so that they can pass along a few morsels of information. Additionally, you can infuse your written menu with little factoids about ingredient sourcing and preparation.

The second big lesson to takeaway pertains to regional specificity. If you can't be *authentically local* – a highly buzzed hospitality term – then this is the next best thing. For example, how can an Italian restaurant in, say, Seattle be locally authentic to its namesake? Instead of this outlet flying the broad banner of just Italian food, why don't the operator and chef plan a menu solely around Trentino cuisine (that is, Alpine fare from the north of the country)?

As we learned from our trip to Eataly, a Sicilian marinara can have vastly different ingredients than tomato sauces from other regions. Some recipes even call for the inclusion of almond paste. The same goes for cheeses, wines, meats and literally everything else that you'd want to put in your mouth. Nor is this a phenomenon exclusive to the diverse regions of Italy. For example, Provençal and Savoyard cuisines are as distinct as oranges and grapefruits.

The Wine Windows of Florence

Have you heard about the little wine holes in Florence and, to a lesser extent, in other Italian cities? It's a humbling story that has emerged out of the pandemic and yet one more reason to visit this illustrious Renaissance center.

Even with all our contemporary influences, people still like to drink just as they did millennia ago, especially during a pandemic when other pastimes are restricted. Large enough to slide a glass of wine through but maintain social distancing, these fun *buchette del vino* were first installed during a 17th century bubonic plague outbreak as a means to give Tuscans a much-needed hit of Sangiovese while limiting direct human contact. Since then, they've largely remained shuttered, generating only a fleeting glimpse from tourists as they saunter off to the next art museum with gelato in hand.

These windows help to transform the wine sold from simple beverage consumption into an entire drinking experience. While we are not advocating you drill a giant hole in the exterior wall of your restaurant to set up your own little wine hole, understanding the inherent value of creating unique and memorable experiences is what will help you increase alcohol revenues in the months and years ahead.

This is another example of *l'ambiente del vino* at work, where it's not about just the purple fluid itself or the process by which it's made but the where, when and how it's enjoyed. You can pop the top off the most expensive Super Tuscan, but it will taste wildly different if you're alone watching a sports game versus if you are appreciating a romantic summer evening while seated out on a medieval piazza.

How do you create your own magical experience? The answer is different for every restaurant, and that's entirely the point in that there's room for grow for every business. Maybe you excel by offering a variety of different tastings to highlight some of the more unique winery partnerships you've formed over the years. Perhaps it's creating a strong point by differentiation by only offering vintages that cannot be found in a liquor store or focusing on a hyper-regional subset of producers while also utilizing esoteric glassware to visually drive the message home. The wine windows of Florence have garnered social media acclaim and are now specifically sought out for their uniqueness.

CELEBRATIONS

Champagne

"I drink Champagne on only two occasions: when I'm in love and when I'm not," remarked Coco Channel. In most bars and restaurants, when it comes to the bubbly, Champagne represents the status quo for taste and class. We see no reason why your servers shouldn't be able to easily help patrons with their sparkling wine selections and convince them of this elixir's worth.

For most, Champagne is an expensive and sugary treat, served in fancy tall and thin glasses otherwise known as flutes. The backstory is, of course, far from boring.

First off, you and your team should know how sparkling wines are produced. This is done by bottling regular wine with lightly pressed grapes so that the skins don't become a factor and bestow their colors onto the end result (for 'white' sparkling wines at least). Then, a little bit of extra yeast and rock sugar are added so that a *secondary fermentation* process occurs as the fungus feasts on the simple carbohydrates, thus creating alcohol and carbon dioxide gas.

Centered on the Marne River around the towns of Reims and Épernay roughly two hours' drive east of Paris, the Champagne growing region traditionally uses the Pinot Noir, Pinot Meunier and Chardonnay grapes in the production of its bubbly varietals. As one of the most northern appellations, this means finicky summer conditions and an early harvest. And for the record, only sparkling wines made in this area can technically be called Champagne, even though many use the two terms interchangeably.

The reason why the Champagne region became famous for its sparkling wines is due to a longstanding rivalry with Burgundy, whereby winemaking houses in the former decided to bow out from the race and differentiate its viticultural enterprises by focusing on said bubbly concoctions. Stemming from this initial divesture came about many of the table names we use today: Veuve Clicquot, Moët & Chandon, Pommery, Dom Pérignon, Laurent-Perrier, Louis Roederer and Taittinger among others. As is customary for all major growing regions, there's a controlling body to ensure adherence to quality production standards and to grade the final vintages in accordance with the classic system of Grand Cru, Premier Cru and Deuxième Cru.

Aside from any classifications or a customer's previous knowledge of one branded house or another, what's most important with Champagne is to meet one's desire for a dry or a sweet bottle. This is determined by the amount of sugar added prior to the secondary fermentation and the residual amount after this process has finished as follows:

- *Brut Nature*: zero, 0-3g/L
- *Extra Brut*: very raw, 0-6g/L
- *Brut*: raw, 0-12g/L
- *Extra Sec*: very dry, 12-17g/L
- *Sec*: dry, 17-32g/L
- *Demi-Sec*: semi-sweet, 32-50g/L
- *Doux*: very sweet, 50+g/L

There's a lot more going on which factors into the taste of sparkling wines. Aside from anything terroir-related, the finest Champagnes have specific vintage years; many do not because they are blends. The rule of thumb is that these wines drink best ten years after the year on the label. Moreover, some believe that Champagne fermented in magnums taste better because of reduced surface area. All these factoids should serve as good fodder for an upsell.

As a final visual, imagine yourself witnessing the time-honored Champagne tradition of *sabrage*. The adjacent table orders an expensive bottle of sparkling wine and, instead of simply popping the top, in one fluid stroke the server slashes the head of the bottle with the blunt end of a saber (or another readily available large knife). Talk about a surprise to add to the overall experience; it might even be enough to push you over the edge and compel you to order your own bottle!

Celebrations and Anchor Pricing

Let's explore the concept of anchor pricing and how you can use it to maximize your beverage sales for any time there's a special occasion and the opportunity to move an expensive bottle. A form of cognitive bias, anchoring is when a person is influenced or nudged towards a particular outcome or decision based upon a previously introduced point of reference.

With applications throughout behavioral economics, the 'pricing' comes when applying this concept to all manner of purchasable goods.

As a foremost travel-related example, consider a two-part thought experiment. In the first part, subjects were asked to choose between two different all-inclusive trips: four nights in Paris or four nights in Rome, both at the same fictitious price of $999. Barring personal or nationalistic preferences for either city within a sample group, the results were more or less an even split. Now for the second part, subjects were asked to choose between those same two $999 Parisian and Roman vacations, but there was a third option thrown in – Rome a la carte for $499.

In this latter case, the overwhelmingly favored choice was the all-inclusive Rome trip. The rationale here is that the cheaper, a la carte alternative to the same city offered a reasonable comparison or 'anchor' through which to see the value of the more expensive Roman trip. Paris had no such analog and thus participants were less able to accurately assess the $999 cost to go to the French capital.

A more quotidian example would be your run-of-the-mill Starbucks coffee break where you must choose between a Tall, Grande and Venti (excluding the Trenta which is only really there for coffeeholics). Amongst these three options, the most commonly chosen size is the Grande – the middle choice – because it is deemed the best value relative to both extremes.

Exporting this principle to wine, what should be apparent is that ordering matters. The first price that customers see will set the tone for the rest of the menu. Similarly, the more luxurious and more expensive end of your wine list also matters insofar as determining the perceived value of all those possible choices in the middle. In other words, if you want people to pony up for a bottle of Dom Pérignon, you may want to add an even more prestigious sparkler in the adjacent space on the menu so that both bottles are immediately comparable to each other.

There are numerous other subtle and overt ways that anchor pricing can help you craft a beverage menu that cajole guests towards certain choices.

Wine and Weddings

Thus far, we've discussed primarily direct-to-consumer wine sales – a couple, a table or someone sitting at the bar, with the server as the main conduit. Event sales are a totally different animal as the buyer's priorities are more cost-conscious while you have different inventory or logistical requirements. The best way to devise your wine plan for group events – as part of the overall beverage strategy – is to start with weddings because almost all of them have wine.

Unlike a restaurant meal where the beverage selection is a front seat driver of the overall experience, for events like a wedding, alcohol and wine often take a backseat. To understand this better, put yourself in the bride and groom's shoes during the venue selection and planning process. The location, availability, ambiance, venue capacity, hotel room pricing and space rental all typically take precedence before food and beverage enters the picture. Then they might go through a site visit and the banqueting food options with samples. Only after all those priorities have been checked off does alcohol and the wine selection enter the picture.

Not only is the budget working against your upselling abilities at this point, but so are the mentalities of the wedding party. The assumption is more than likely to be that the host's guests don't have an advanced knowledge of wine; a basic, palpable red and white will suffice. Why spend any more than they have to? Yet, at the same time, the bride and groom don't want to appear cheap, so the two wines shouldn't be the most popular ones in the liquor store in order to avoid on-the-spot price comparisons. Rarely either will wedding planners select vintages from your core wine list. Instead, they'll work off a catering menu, creating a short wine list unique for the event.

These factors taken into account, the selling falls upon your catering staff and sales team who seldom receive bespoke training or are not as inherently knowledgeable as your servers and sommeliers. Moreover, the desire for a once-in-a-lifetime occasion begs for the creation of a private label wine.

Obviously, there are lots of obstacles in maximizing wine revenues from a wedding, let alone any other event where the beverages aren't a top consideration. With weddings as a core scenario then branching out to anniversary parties, reunions, meetings, corporate retreats and other common event RFPs you are likely to receive, we can now create some guidelines for your event wine strategy.

It begins your merchant and wholesaler relationship. Ask them about wines that cannot be directly compared with what a consumer can find on the shelf. What can you get that's decent at a bulk discount price? Would they be prepared to conduct training for your sales and banqueting teams, not just your bar and waitstaff?

As for the vintages chosen, stay conservative and mainstream. Even if a cheap label is offered from, say, Serbia, this should be avoided as it's too esoteric for some minds. Think wines from California, France and Italy, while you can also consider ones from Argentina, Chile or South Africa provided the varietal is an international flight or stereotypical of the region. And the taste profile should be neutral so that it pairs with any dish on the prix fixe menu.

If the bride and groom want a bubbly for a toast, keep a Prosecco available as Champagnes purchased in quantity will be unaffordable for most, thus eliminating the possibility of a sale altogether. Sometimes, it will be deemed appropriate to have a higher caliber selection for the head table, for which choosing off the standard restaurant wine list can be an option. In this case, just be sure to serve this premium wine decanted to obscure the differentiated product from what others receive to avoid comparison.

Next comes total quantity per a BEO and stocking. A rule of thumb is one bottle per person for budget purposes, plus additional wine for the cocktail reception. Serve the same wine in this pre-dinner function as you would for dinner to avoid confusion.

While weddings are a unique and lucrative opportunity for a hotel, every other event can attain healthy beverage sales if the sales team is trained, and the menu is designed appropriately for the customer's specific needs. Finally, there will be exceptions to this approach, so qualification and flexibility are also important much all other aspects of the sales process.

Happy Liberalia

There is a defunct Roman holiday – the Liberalia – that occurs on the day of St. Patrick's Day. While the modern leprechaun is keen on beer, the

Roman counterpart upheld wine as its hallowed libation, with a lesson to be had from this comparison.

Without going into details about the weird and hypersexualized rituals that the ancient Italians had for the Liberalia, what's interesting is that it was not just a celebration to honor the god of viticulture – that is, Liber Pater, and not Bacchus or Dionysus who were the Roman gods of wine and who were honored during the Bacchanalia held annually around Halloween. The Liberalia also served as a coming-of-age ceremony for teenagers; thereafter they would be deemed responsible for adult tasks and for conducting themselves in a civilized manner.

Unless, say, picking up a couple dozen Budweiser or Coors Light, genuine deference for wine requires a likewise maturation of one's own intellect to fully appreciate the complexity of this age-old elixir. Part of wine's allure is that it is a sophisticated beverage, and certainly much more than just a 'basic' source of alcohol-induced contentment.

The word 'basic' deserves some unpacking because even though they may be similarly priced, no two wines, beers, cocktails or spirits should ever be deemed as interchangeable in the customer's mind. What will drive your beverage sales to reach new heights is the work you do to prevent any perception of commoditization. It's an important note because if all alcoholic offers are directly transposable without any semblance of exceptionality or exclusivity, then your guests will always lean heavily towards those with the lowest price.

Thus, the Liberalia and the deep veneration that Roman society had for wine offer a profound marketing lesson that can be deployed ubiquitously. To stave off any perceived commoditization, you must present an emotional commitment and a passion for your wears. By treating each liquor with respect insofar as caring to know a bit about its origins, its manufacturing process and a few specific tasting notes, this knowledge will be paid forward. It requires a wholehearted cultural adjustment.

Happy Winesday

One common practice at a restaurant is to devote a given day of the week or period of each day – otherwise known as happy hour – to a special promotion, either in the form of unique offerings or unbeatable deals. While this a good start for boosting those slow midweek periods, numerous other eateries already have these types of programs in place.

And when everyone else is doing something like this, how can you stand out by directly imitating your competitors? You can't, unless you change the rules slightly or design a promotion that is truly differentiated from what's expected.

Whether your promotion falls on a Wednesday or not as 'Winesday' references, a catchy title alone can pay off through its heightened memorability, regardless of the customer savings on display. Aside from the pun itself, a phrasing such as 'Happy Winesday' also implies a more elevated experience, one that's a celebration of this millennia-old beverage. To live up to this expectation, you must think not just in terms of a monetary incentive such as 'half off wine by the glass' but in terms of how you can transform such a promotion into an experiential event.

While reduced prices on alcohol may spur someone to buy another round or have a glass with a meal when not originally intended, it's not adding depth or another dimension to the overall meal experience. However, when you build a vino-centric calendar of events with, for example, small glass flights, tastings themed by growing region, supporting materials describing the flavor profiles or wine origins, thoughtful cuisine pairings, exclusive imports and even guided tasting by a professional sommelier, you are augmenting a promotion with customer education and fonder appreciation.

100-Point Wines

What's in a number? More specifically, what does '100' mean on a rating scale? Typically, something that reaches triple digits like this is equivalent to a perfect score; the best there is.

When it comes to wine, numbers are important. Those who are aficionados understand ratings issued by *Wine Spectator*, *Wine Advocate* or others. New entrants are also coming onto the scene to guide beginner oenophiles on their quest for grape enlightenment; try playing around with the mobile app Vivino.

Each of these well-known resources ranks vintages every year based upon their staffs' finely tuned palates. The rating scales used tend to be logarithmic whereby an 88-scoring – while quite acceptable for the average person – is the equivalent of plonk for the calibrated tongue. When a wine is ranked 100, it is not just a good wine; it is one of the very best in the world. And if you think about the tens of thousands of vineyards and the multiple varieties sold by each winery, it is incredible to think that a 100 rating is annually bestowed on a handful of bottles at most. In fact, a 100-point wine is so rare that even to drink one is a very special occasion – perhaps one should wear a tuxedo or evening gown for the occasion.

Given their rarity, few restaurants offer 100-rated bottles on their wine list. If they do, fewer places still have more than one or two, and in very limited quantity. On top of all that, with prices soaring into the high triple and quadruple (and quintuple!) figures, there are only a morsel of consumers willing to fork over the necessary cash for such an indulgence. In this sense, a restaurant's 100-point wines are not really for drinking, but instead a cachet to propel the entire wine list into the limelight.

Hence, while drinking 100-point wines is on our bucket list in perpetuity, we don't actively seek them out on a regular basis as we would go broke within a matter of weeks. Instead, we use the presence of said bottles as a barometer for the rest of the cellar. Much like how anchor pricing works but for wine caliber, a respectable collection of 100-pointers indicates a commendable selection of everything else.

When you extrapolate this inductive reasoning, it's easy to see how a well-curated wine list can serve as an alternative promotional vehicle for an establishment; to be renowned for your cuisine as well as your wine. Moreover, when a restaurant has a vast store of 100-rated bottles, not just a handful, it greatly augments the wine's marketing power to the point where the cellar becomes an attraction in its own right.

A recent trip to Crystal Springs Resort in Hamburg, New Jersey, just outside of New York City and its Restaurant Latour (*Wine Spectator* Grand Award Winner for many years) provided a firsthand experience with one of the finest cellars on the continent. Here, wine is not just a computerized bin number (there are close to 150,000 bottles in stock), but a true passion. Here you will find over 200 different 100-pointers and they are all for sale with more than one of each available. The cellar itself is built like a museum – a true *cave à vin*.

This isn't not just wine appreciation on steroids, its oenophile heaven.

And in northern New Jersey no less! The strategy here is that Crystal Springs Resort has clearly levered its world-class wine cellar as a prime differentiator. In its competitive market for meetings and groups business, the hotel's wine list serves as a core asset to draw this segment and other corporate social events. In this case, the wine isn't merely an adjunct to the restaurant, but it acts as its own amenity whereby guests can tour the cellar at their own convenience, independent of whether they are about to dine or not. With a valuation at over $30 million, the property's cave à vin is unforgettable, which plays a significant role in both repeat visits and positive word of mouth.

CONCLUSION

Wine Needs Education

There are two major trends that restaurateurs and hoteliers should be aware of that may negatively impact wine sales over the next two decades. First, the younger generations – millennials and centennials – have less disposable income compared to their parents. And second, global wine prices are continually inching upwards due to a variety of macroeconomic forces including increased worldwide demand, climate change interrupting supply and monetary inflation driving investors into asset classes such as art or fine wine.

Together, these two factors – less money overall and higher average prices – mean that young people will come to see wine purchases as an increasingly expensive gambit relative to other cheaper forms of alcoholic consumption such as beer or hard seltzers. They will thus be less inclined to try a bottle and ingratiate themselves in the vast vinicultural world that helps keep restaurants afloat. Without steady exposure to wine in one's formative years, there will be little to no emotional connection to wine when one has income to spare later on.

Why is a personal bond important? Because with most non-essential items, a product's value is largely derived from what people are willing to pay for it. This is particularly true for those bottles at the rarified end of the spectrum where distinguishing their remarkable flavor profiles requires training and a development of one's palate over time. Remove the training through lack of exposure to entry-level then mid-level producers in one's 20s and 30s, and apathy towards fine wine is what follows.

At the microeconomic level, a person without a core emotional connection to wine will need a lot more cajoling to opt for a $100 bottle instead of a $50 one. Without a gradual introduction to higher tiers and better quality – as incentivized by reasonable prices that are not entirely exclusionary – the hefty price tag on a menu becomes all the harder to justify. We may end up with a whole generation that is largely indifferent to how great your restaurant's cellar is and unwilling to pay three or four times the markup for your corkage services because they have next to zero passion for fine wine.

Of course, there will always be affluent patrons who can afford something off the top shelf or those who are prone to conspicuous consumption. These customers may start to wane until one day you are scratching your head wondering why your wine sales are so abysmal. Instead, you may see an upward trend in wine by the glass, craft beer or specialty cocktail purchases, with a net lower alcohol-per-person spend.

This is, of course, highly speculative but nevertheless something you should ponder. What can you do about it? Or more specifically, how can you imbue a sense of passion into these cash-strapped youngsters so that they can inevitably see the light?

The first step towards appreciation is awareness. After all, how can someone care about something if they don't know it exists or why it's significant? This means injecting a bit of education into your wine list by perhaps explaining the grape varietals and their archetypical flavor profiles or talking about the region where your partnered wineries are located. It can be in writing or taught to your servers so they can convey it succinctly in person. Even though we're talking macroeconomic trends, one restaurant can make a difference.

As an example, for a property out in British Columbia where we were serving as asset managers, we wanted to create a sense of meaning for their wine cellar, so the first step was to theme the offerings. With this province in Canada becoming a hotbed of some truly spectacular drops, we set about ensuring that over 90% of the inventory was local, then embellished this throughout our marketing presentation as well as through a visual guide at the beginning of the cellar binder. All staff went through a full month of intermittent training to understand what makes the province's wines and winemakers special, as well as how the menu reflected this.

This was a monstrous amount of work to get it all up and running, but the result was that customers understood this property and its signature restaurant as a purveyor of the 'Best of British Columbia', coming specifically for some of the more obscure or cult labels. And upon seating, many patrons delighted in perusing the full list, deepening their personal connection to wine the more they read.

Finding a Wine List Time Capsule

A friend's cookbook gift unearthed an astonishing bonus – a 60-year-old wine list from a luxury Caribbean resort (The Dorado Beach Resort in San Juan, Puerto Rico). At the time, wine habits consisted of only red or white, while the Californian wine industry was basically a volume business of jug wines at low prices. Drinking fine wine was clearly a fringe experience reserved for the finest restaurants and aristocratic palates. Oh, how times have changed!

This primary source indicates how did they sell wine in the 1950s and 1960s. Significantly, it can help you to develop a trendline for how to sell more wine the future.

First, in this 60-year-old list there is a detailed description about each of the types of wines with grapes and growing regions. Rarely have we seen such a voluminous text inclusion on any modern wine list. Next, within each wine type and region, bottles are sorted in price order with key features identified. Many half bottles are available as well, far more than what would be currently offered. The products available include only two American vintages while all the remaining offerings are from France and Germany. Lastly, there is a final section entitled, 'Some of the Rarest Wines in the World' with an introductory paragraph that makes each feel more like circus oddities than exquisite drinking experiences.

Today, North American tastes for wine are far more educated and the array of available product options has expanded exponentially. A typical wine list at a fine dining establishment will run many pages, potentially intimidating to the novice drinker but also intriguing to those who are interested in exploring the many facets of this miraculous liquid.

What is most interesting about this unearthed wine capsule is the pricing. The lowest prices for full bottles are the two rosés, both at $3.60. The most expensive was a Château Margaux 1929 for $35. But you could have saved money and bought the 1964 vintage for only $18. Interestingly, the ratio of most expensive to cheapest was roughly 10:1.

One can't help but note the significant rise in pricing for today's ultra-high-end wines; we are probably at a range-price ratio of nearly 1000:1 by now. Just examine your latest wine list. If your lowest offering is, say, $35, what do you offer for $175 or $350? Like everything in life, the best continues to be sought out with vigorous demand and the scarce are only becoming scarcer. Some things change for the better, though. Just consider the shock of not having Californian wines readily available for purchase (at least in a North American capacity). Ask people what they thought of

Californian wines in 1966 and they might scrunch their noses. Nowadays, they lick their lips.

In the past two decades, we have seen a similar growth and acceptance of Argentine, Australian, Chilean, New Zealand and South African wines. What will the next two decades bring us? Oregon now makes Pinot Noirs that rival Napa in all but prestige and price. The Finger Lakes region in New York is experimenting with Baco Noir to elevate that varietal above jug status. Lebanon and Northern Israel are bringing vinicultural recognition back to its roots in the Levant. Mexico has a small but burgeoning wine culture in Baja California. Brazil has the Rio Grande do Sul region that already makes a few fine Merlots and sparkling wines. Eastern European nations like Hungary, Romania, Georgia and Bulgaria are also emerging from their communist doldrums to globally export some truly delightful bottles.

Lastly, what can we extrapolate about wine prices in the coming decades? If the past 50 years have been any indication, expect fine wine prices to only go higher. And this makes sense as worldwide appreciation increases – an effect most pronounced by the recent proliferation of Chinese demand for fine wines. What will happen if wine reaches similar levels of popularity in India, another country of over a billion potential buyers? That 1000:1 ratio might reach 2000:1 or more by the time our tongue (our wallet!) gives out.

The world of wine is only getting larger and more elaborate. The more you learn about this beverage, the more you realize you don't know anything yet. If you plan to use this beverage as a means for more restaurant revenues and increased customer satisfaction, you best stay on top of the trends as you never know where the next big thing will come from.

The Future of Wine

As 3D printing technologies gain scale and maturity, we're starting to see accurate recreations of foods such as pizzas, chocolate chip cookies and even steaks from lab-grown meat tissue. Will there be a time when something as intricate as a specific wine vintage can also be produced from such a device?

We are a long way's off from the food replicators in *Star Trek* but imagine the possibilities. Commercially installing a wine machine of this nature would offer your restaurant a whole world of wineries at the push of a button. The inklings are there with the advent of airtight, self-dispensing machines like the Wineemotion™.

In the future, with enough science behind the exact classifications of the full array of molecules and their concentrations contained in a 100-point Bordeaux or Californian cult favorite, such a formula could be put on the blockchain and sold up as a proprietary NFT to a limited buyer pool of restaurants eager for a point of differentiation. Then there are the opportunities for 3D-printed vertical tastings or giving customers the opportunity to blend their own glass on the spot.

This could be like the Coca-Cola Freestyle soda fountains currently in movie theaters and theme parks, only instead of choosing to mix lemon and raspberry Diet Coke you've narrowed your blend down to a 2019 Pinot Noir from Burgundy and a 2021 Pinot Noir from Willamette.

Some would consider such a blend to be blasphemous, but then again it was only a generation ago when it was anathema to switch from Coca-Cola to Pepsi. Time's change, and the centuries-long trend is moving towards more variety and more choice for customers. What starts as a novelty can quickly become mainstream. While we're still quite some time off from being able to use 3D printers to make anything better than pure plonk, if there's a will, there's a way. History has proven to never bet against technology.

It's great to ruminate on the distant century when we're all shadows, but what's the lesson for the present? Think about the value of an item – any item, a specific wine bottle or otherwise – in the face of commoditization and other deflationary forces. Generally speaking, said item loses value until it finds a natural equilibrium with supply.

The prospects of 3D printing will eventually pose the same challenge for the wine industry. With the ability to make a basic wine product on the spot, it increases access and lowers the costs per unit, allowing restaurants to incentivize patrons by undercutting competitors who are still opting for the traditional supply chain. And if it's shown that such machines can create a quality product, then all bets are off.

In the face of commoditization driving down real beverage prices, the answer is to create appeal in other aspects of your restaurant – the ambiance, the place settings, the service, the food, the knowledge of your staff, the recommended pairings and the experience. But if you've been reading this book and got this far, then you'll know that that is what wine has always been about.

Once you get beyond garbage wine which gives the drinker heartburn and headaches, most people are statistically horrible at distinguishing one bottle from another. Even professional tasters do not get it right all the time. In one experiment, white wine was colored red, and the pros didn't notice, instead assigning quintessential red-wine adjectives to the trick white.

The point here is that wine is as much about perception as it is the chemical attributes that come together to elicit a given flavor and bouquet. That won't change even as the technology does. You could put the same wine into two different bottles then charge $50 and $200 respectively for each, and the more expensive one will be deemed in aggregate as having the better taste.

For your purposes, wine is a tool to help keep the lights on at a dining outlet by drumming up more beverage sales. For the customer, wine is an instrument to enhance the experience, due to its alcohol content and meal complement as well as the perception of sophistication it generates and helping set the mood.

This is where we leave you. However much wine's journey – from vine to cask to bottle to your tongue – gets reduced to a science that can potentially be duplicated by a 3D printer in a century's time, the experience that wine creates will ultimately remain an artform.

TERMINOLOGY

We could write several dozen pages of wine terminology and definitions. Here are some that we hope you will find useful.

ABV: Alcohol by volume.

AC or AOC: Appellation Controlée or Appellation d'Origine Controlée, referring to the location in France where the wine grapes are grown. There are 363 AOCs in that country for wine as well as for spirits. Similar regionalization exists in other countries.

AVA: American Viticultural Area, used in the United States in a similar manner as the French system, with the national differences beyond the scope of any guest-facing sales conversation.

Appassimento: A grape drying technique to increase the residual sugar levels prior to maceration and fermentation.

Astringency: A flavor profile common for highly tannic red wine where the drinker is left with a dry, rough, puckering mouth sensation.

Bottle Sizes: 750ml is the standard bottle size; a Magnum is 1.5L (two bottles); a Double Magnum is 3L; a Jeroboam is 4.5L (six standard bottles). There are even larger sizes, although they are rare. A Piccolo or Split (generally of Champagne) is one-quarter of a bottle or 187ml.

BEO: Banquet Event Order, specifying all the details for an event.

Breathing: The process that allows air to reach the wine, typically by decanting. Generally, this isn't necessary for white wines. Older red wines that have been laid down in a temperature-controlled cellar for five years or longer need time to breathe and fully evolve the flavor. Often such wines will change completely inside of 30 minutes after opening.

Brix: The measurement of the sugar content of grapes at maturity.

Brut: Translated from French as 'crude', typically describing a very dry Champagne.

BTG: Wine poured and sold 'by the glass'.

Champagne: A sparkling wine made exclusively in the Champagne district of France. Only wines from this region can be called Champagne. If they follow the process of Champagne but are not from the region they are referred to as Méthode Champenoise.

Château Bottled: For French wine, it means wine was bottled in this location.

Cicerone: The term for a beer sommelier, pronounced the Italian way as 'chee-che-*roh*-ne'.

Claret: Another term for a red Bordeaux wine, typically used in Great Britain.

Color: Red or white or rosé (pink), color is used as a further descriptor of the wine, as in clear or cloudy, dark or light.

Decanting: The process of pouring a bottle of wine into an open container or decanter. Careful decanting allows sediment to remain in the bottle. Decanting permits the wine to breathe, changing the flavor profile through oxidation.

DISCUS: Distilled Spirits Council of the United States.

DOC or DOCG: Classifications of highest quality Italian wines, standing for Denominazione di Origine Controllata and Denominazione di Origine Controllata e Garantita.

DRC: Domaine de la Romanée-Conti refers to a tiny region in Burgundy, France that produces the most expensive and coveted wines in the world. Its name comes from the most famous vineyard, Romanée-Conti, and includes the almost-as-spectacular vineyards of La Tâche, Richebourg, Romanée-Saint-Vivant, Échezeaux and Montrachet.

Dry: A description of wine where the sugar has mostly converted to alcohol and thus there is little sweetness.

F&B: Food and Beverage; a common shorthand for the hotel industry to demarcate this operation from others within the same building.

Fortified: A wine that has been strengthened by the addition of a high-proof spirit. Typically, examples are Sherry or Port. This fortification increases the alcohol content from 14% to 18%.

Foxy: Wine made from native North American grapes known as fox grapes. Usually, a derogatory term as the aroma and taste does not compare to hybrid grapes usually found in wines.

Grand Cru: The top level of wines from the Burgundy region of France; lesser quality is Premiere Cru.

Hybrid Grapes: Grapes resulting from a cross of native American with European counterparts, often resulting in a fine wine.

Ice Wine: Wine that is made from grapes harvested after the first frost. This results in a very sweet product typically consumed after dinner. Any grape can be harvested in this fashion, but typically a Vidal or Riesling varietal is utilized. More recently Cabernet Franc and Cabernet Sauvignon have delivered excellent ice wine.

IGT: Indicazione Geografica Tipica; used for Italian wines as a marker for high quality albeit attained using varietals or processes that are non-traditional for the region.

IPA: India Pale Ale; a typically dark, stinky and especially hoppy style of beer that also skews higher on the ABV.

Judgement of Paris: May 24, 1976, the day that Napa wineries (Chateau Montelena and Stags' Leap) beat their French counterparts in a Paris blind taste testing. The result opened the door for New World wine appreciation.

Jug Wines: Basic wines with a negative connection, the name comes from being sold in large bottles as large as a gallon.

Kabinett: The first level of German wine quality above table and quality wines. In increasing order of weight or alcohol and sugar, these are Kabinett, Spätlese and Auslese (there are multiple levels of Auslese wines with even higher levels of sugar).

Kosher Wine: Wine that is produced in accordance with Jewish dietary laws so that observant Jews are be permitted to drink it. Wine of this type are used in several Jewish ceremonies, typically as a Kiddush or blessing.

Light Wine: There is no specific definition for a light wine. A Pinot Noir is considered a light red wine; a Pinot Grigio is considered a light white wine. Alcohol levels for a light wine are typically less than 14%. This refers to body and is not to be confused with low-alcohol wines.

Master of Wine: An individual who has completed the very comprehensive Master of Wine course. By many considered a 'doctor of wine', they typically add the designation MW after their name.

Must: Crushed grapes in the first stage of winemaking.

Noble Rot: English for *botrytis cinerea*, a fungus that attacks grapes, dehydrating them to result in a higher sweetness level for the wine as well as the production of glycerol.

Oenophile: A wine connoisseur, with 'oenophilia' denoting the concept of 'loving wine'.

Orange Wine: Also known as amber wine or skin-contact wine, this color of wine is produced by leaving the skins of white wine grapes to ferment with the juice instead of removing them, essentially making white wine in the same manner as red wine.

Plonk: A slang term for cheap, often foul-tasting wine.

QR: Quick Ready; a standardized matrix or two-dimensional barcode that can be read by a phone's camera to direct users to a specific webpage or app screen.

Remuage: The periodic twisting or shaking of a Champagne bottle to dislodge sediment as the product ages, as inscribed by the Méthode Champenoise.

RFP: Request for Proposal; a common name used in meetings, events and banqueting to indicate that a planner is ready to negotiate or receive a quote from a venue.

Riedel: Recognized as one of the expert manufacturers of wine glasses, typically considered the gold standard of glassware.

Robert Parker: A highly regarded wine expert whose ratings (on a scale to 100) are generally taken as gospel insofar as the quality ranking for a wine/vintage.

Rosé: A pink wine creased by minimizing the period during which red wine grape skins are allowed to ferment in the must.

Super Tuscan: Referring to an inventive style originating outside of the Chianti Classico zone, these red wines are rich and full-bodied, age well, and have nicely integrated tannins and spice from oak. The original Super Tuscan, Sassicaia, made near the town of Bolgheri, is considered one of the best wines in the world and launched the IGT denomination.

Tannin: A phenolic ingredient in grape skins that produces astringency and complexity. Tannins fade with time in the bottle.

Tawny: Port and other red wines that have lost their red color and turned brown.

Thief: A wine thief is a tubular instrument that is used to steal wine from a barrel to test it through various stages of maturity.

USP: Unique Selling Proposition, representing the elevator pitch or the core reason for a customer to buy a product.

Varietal: A grape cultivar, with the specific genetics determining skin coloration, fruit yield, sugar content, phenolic compound concentrations, adverse weather resistance, time to maturation, and the ratios of acetic, citric and malic acids.

Vineyard: Land where the grapevines are grown.

VQA: Vintner's Quality Alliance; used in the Canadian provinces of British Columbia and Ontario to identify that the wine is produced from grapes grown in that province.

Wine Key: Another name for a corkscrew.

Winery: The place where wine is processed, first into tanks and then barrels. After barrel aging (for most wines), wines are then bottled.

Wine Spectator: A highly respected wine magazine. Their rankings are highly influential.

WSET: The Wine & Spirit Education Trust provides three levels of course instruction on wines, along with a series of specialty courses for specific producing nations and other diplomas in spirits or sake.

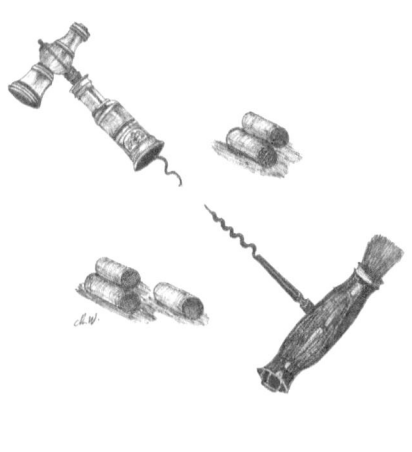

ACKNOWLEDGEMENTS

Our wine journey has been one of constant tasting and discussions. We don't just drink wine (as well as the occasional spirit), we savor everyone who has joined us for a glass, discussing the beverage's merits while comparing it to glasses we have had in the past. Through this process, we document our consumption using the Vivino app which allows us to catalog our progress. As of this writing, we have collectively reviewed some 3,000 different wines, with this number continuing to grow.

As mentioned, wine serves as a catalyst. Along the way, we have engaged with several individuals who we would like to mention here (in alphabetical order): Richard Anderson, Svetlana Atcheva, Rupert Brendon, Chef Daniel Bruce, Keith Edwards, Kevin Haverty Jr., Drew Innes, Suzanne Janke, Dale Jeffries, Stephen G. Johnston, Matthew Jukes, Amy McCandlish,

Shannon McCallum, Milton Mednick, Alvin Nirenberg, Steve Ranger, Klaus Tenter, James Tenute, Josef Wagner, Mat Woo and Robby Younes.

And as always, Larry's spouse of over four decades and Adam's mother, Maureen Wright, deserves praise for calmly putting up with our constant arguing and erratic work schedules, not to mention her exceptional illustrations which are integral to this book. We would also like to thank Sam Mogelonsky, Larry's daughter and Adam's sister, for lending her time to crafting this book's amazing cover design.

The hospitality business, which is our core focus, is one of people. Wine is a natural extension, or subset, of being a successful hotelier and restaurateur. We are honored to have so many friends in this business who provide an endless stream of ideas for us to write about. To all those colleagues and clients who we've had the pleasure of knowing over the years, we sincerely thank you for making us the humble (and hopefully more knowledgeable!) people that we are today.

ABOUT THE AUTHORS

Larry and Adam Mogelonsky are a father-son consulting team constantly in search of ways to perfect the hotel and service experience. Sometimes that means incorporating new technology or new amenities, but often it means optimizing the assets a property already has and getting back to the basics of working in a service culture. Very often, this includes F&B, which typically means wine management.

After a formal education in engineering and business plus a stint as a brand manager at Procter & Gamble, Larry's first brush with the industry was during his half-dozen years at a top ten advertising agency where he was the team leader for the Four Seasons Hotels & Resorts account. Smitten with the hospitality bug, Larry then founded LMA Communications in 1991 as a boutique firm specializing in hotels and tourism with clients across the globe. Since its inception, LMA has been recognized with over one hundred awards from HSMAI (Hospitality Sales and Marketing Association International) for its creativity and strategic business acumen, as well as being awarded TravelClick's Worldwide e-Marketer of the Year.

Before joining his father in the family business, Adam attained an undergraduate degree in pre-medicine and was working as a physiotherapist for several years. Starting as a junior copywriter and digital strategist right at the time when social media was becoming a major marketing platform for brands, Adam rose over the years to become an account director for LMA's various hotel clients.

Selling LMA, Larry and Adam jointly formed Hotel Mogel Consulting as a way of helping solve critical issues and working closer with property owners, operators and industry suppliers. Together, they strive to offer the best strategies for their clients, all while never losing sight of the core drivers of a great hotel experience and what will lead to long-term success.

Concurrent to their consultancy practice, both Larry and Adam are active hospitality writers, thought leaders and public speakers. Over the past decade, they have published over 1,100 unique articles in *eHotelier*, *HOTELS Magazine*, *Hotel-Online*, *Hotel News Now*, *Hotel Executive*, *Hotel Interactive*, *HospitalityNet*, *Hotel Technology News*, *Today's Hotelier*, *Canadian Lodging News* and *Hotelier Magazine*. Twice monthly, their newsletter, aptly named *The Hotel Mogel*, reaches thousands of senior managers.

In addition to periodicals, Larry and Adam have published six prior books addressing operational, branding, sales and marketing issues for hoteliers entitled, "Are You an Ostrich or a Llama?" (2012), "Llama Rules" (2013), "Hotel Llama" (2015), "The Llama is Inn" (2017), "The Hotel Mogel" (2018) and "More Hotel Mogel" (2020). All six texts are typically available for sale through Amazon and other booksellers.

As a part of their speaking tour, Larry has been a keynote speaker at worldwide industry conferences including HITEC, BITAC, Hospitality Innovation Planet, BTO Italia, Hawaii Lodging & Tourism Association, Hotel Data Conference, Visit Florida Governor's Conference, Cornell Hotel Research Symposium, HVS Eastern Europe, TTG Travel Experience and Hospitality Day Italia as well as numerous corporate events and university seminars.

Both Larry and Adam reside in Toronto. Larry lives with his wife, Maureen, and their 150-pound Bouvier des Flandres named Hondo, while Adam lives downtown mere blocks from all the greatest hotel and restaurants in this booming city. Contact them at larry@hotelmogel.com or adam@hotelmogel.com.

CHEERS TO ALL!

"Wine is bottled poetry."
– Robert Louis Stevenson

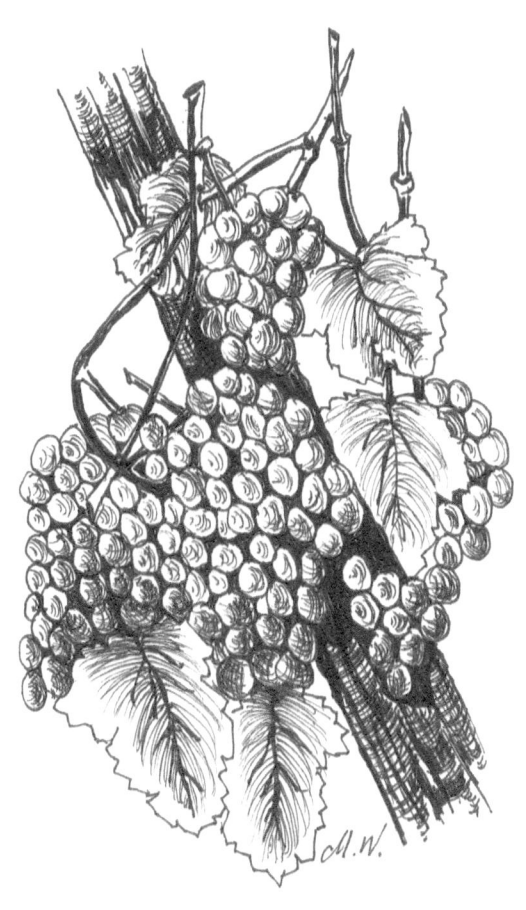